TORY LIVES

BY THE SAME AUTHOR

George Wyndham : A Study in Toryism

Lucius Cary, 2nd Viscount Falkland

From the portrait attributed to Hannemans in the Devonshire Collection

JOHN BIGGS-DAVISON

Tory Lives

From Falkland to Disraeli

LONDON
Putnam & Co. Ltd.
42 GREAT RUSSELL STREET

FIRST PUBLISHED 1952

Printed by The Thanet Press, Union Crescent, Margate

TO
MY MOTHER AND FATHER

"The common problem, yours, mine, everyone's
Is not to fancy what were fair in life,
Provided it could be,—but, finding first
What may be, then find out how to make it fair
Up to our means—a very different thing!
No abstract intellectual plan of Life
Quite irrespective of life's plainest laws,
But one a man, who is a man and nothing more,
May lead within a world which (by your leave)
Is Rome or London—not Fool's paradise."

Robert Browning

"Remember . . ."

Charles the First

PREFACE

I give no list of authorities. A Tory, I am much indebted to the Whig historians. Others have redressed the bias; but their work has not been superseded.

Among those who have encouraged and helped me, I would make grateful mention of my wife and of my sister-in-law, Mrs. George Wyndham, of Orchard Wyndham, also of Mr. Richard Feilden, M.A. (Cantab.), who read the proofs and made several valuable suggestions.

I was emboldened to write these pages by the Tory revival of our day and by the strenuous Tory efforts, in the face of Marxism and misrepresentation, to cast off the sodden incubus of Whiggery.

J. B-D.

Chelsea.
October, 1952.

CONTENTS

ILLUSTRATIONS

TORY LIVES

Introductory Chapter

BENJAMIN DISRAELI ranked the adoption of an English form of constitution by the French "among the prime follies of human conduct", and civil authority will needs be exercised in various ways in different times and different lands. There can be the widest variety of political system without there being any conflict with the law of God or of its lesser reflexion the natural law.

On another occasion Disraeli declared that "society has a soul as well as a body. The traditions of a nation are part of its existence." History and experience teach that the constitution which endures is that which is framed in consonance with the traditions of the people. The English do well to cherish their ancient Monarchy, the Swiss their ancient Republic.

The conservative instinct is a natural instinct. Gilbert wrote that—

> Every boy and every gal
> That's born into the world alive,
> Is either a little Liberal
> Or else a little Conservative.

Rather is every child born a conservative, with a healthy mistrust of innovation. The political animal is torn by two contrary motives: first, the visionary urge to make all things new; second, and more prominent, the aversion from severed roots and the discomfort and suffering which are the companions of change. Whether or not we hear at some stage of our life a call to reform and to rebel, whether or not we respond to that call, the instinct and desire to resist whatever appears to menace our peace or our peace of mind is a desire and an instinct strong in all of us.

In political society, therefore, we find a conservative force and conservative classes, and, where political parties have appeared, they will ordinarily include reactionaries, conservatives and revolutionaries. The reactionary is one who seeks the restoration of an earlier order or class structure; the revolutionary demands the sudden or violent imposition of reforms, and those, independently of his aims and intentions, either provoke reaction or terminate in tyranny; the conservative wisely accepts necessary or unavoidable change and directs it in the path of peaceful reform. He thus forestalls the infructuous misery of revolution and ensures for his society that continuity of growth from which it derives sustenance and strength.

International Communism and international Social Democracy are realities, for they derive from a common Marxist philosophy, whether of the orthodox or some bowdlerized protestant variety, and it has been found possible to set up a Liberal International, for political Liberalism began in circumstances which have visited most Western countries and was inspired by philosophers whose writings are the possession of no single country. But any concept of English or British Conservatism as a national branch of a European or international system is preposterous and nonsensical. The Tory or Conservative Party is either a national party, or it is nothing. It is strictly local, as also practical and pragmatic. Conservative politics are the pursuit of the possible. Conscious of the reality of original sin, knowing that we have no power of ourselves to help ourselves, the Conservative is sceptical of innovation and deferential to those members of his community who are dead or yet unborn. Yet he is zealous to improve what exists and to remove all abuses which are contrary to human dignity and welfare, and which are provocative of revolution.

One advantage of the odd old name of Tory over the later title of Conservative, which dates, significantly enough, from the period of Peel, is that it is not a name for foreign imitation. The opprobrious origin of the designation will be considered later. It is an English origin and although the name has been applied loosely and abusively in the politics of other English-speaking peoples, Toryism is not for export.

The Tories, as a Party, have no ties outside these islands. When the Tory speaks to foreigners or to his fellow-subjects overseas, he speaks as a Briton, not as a Tory; there is no such thing as a Conservative foreign policy. On the other hand, as every Christian has his neighbour, so does every Christian nation, and no study of the origins of Toryism can remain entirely insular. The history of England is older than the history of our Nation State and many Tory traditions are traditions of the whole people and of their Church. They derive from many sources and primarily from Jerusalem and Athens, whence they were borne along the highways of Imperial Rome to the monasteries and manors of Christendom. There they were enlivened by the culture of the barbarians. The roots of the Tory philosophy are medieval and pre-medieval; a national philosophy, it is founded upon the general inheritance of Christendom and the West.

The fundamental difference between modern and medieval society is that the former is primarily secular; the latter was primarily religious. Medieval man related his thought and his work to what the Church taught him of the mind of God. To work was to pray and to pray was to think God's thoughts, within the limits of human imperfection. But though religious, medieval society was not theocratic. The Church and the Papacy might encroach upon the sphere of kings, but kings would ordinarily resist what was plainly an encroachment. Anarchy might place a sceptre in the gift of the Pontiff, but anarchy demands an exception. The Prince for his part would wield the sceptre *sub Deo et sub lege* and the obedience of his subjects was conditional upon the undertakings of the Coronation Oath, the first of which was that the Prince must defend the rights of Holy Church. Medieval monarchy was in a sense contractual; absolute kingship was something later. The picture of two swords which ruled Christian men, that of the Pope and that of the Emperor, did not fade when the Empire was smitten into nations. The idea of a temporal and a spiritual power, each balancing the other, made liberty and progress possible though days were dark.

In a Christian society men are members one of another. Each has his part to play. In medieval times some ploughed, some prayed, and some taught; some plied their craft or trade; some held land and manors from the King, giving him service in return and protection to the people. Property was a trust, and it was to a medieval principle that Disraeli appealed when he declared that "the tenure of property rests upon the performance of duties". Not the religious or the clergy alone, but all had their vocation, and accompanying privileges and obligations.

All was supposed to be done as to God; business was to be governed by justice. There was therefore a just price for goods—economic laws were not allowed to supplant the laws of God—and their quality was as much the concern of the craft guilds as was the wellbeing of the guildsmen. Men were individuals as brethren and sons of God: in that lay their equality, but society was not yet permitted to degenerate into an agglomeration of individuals. Nor was it totalitarian. The spiritual writ of the Church set bounds to regal and feudal power, and baronial exactions and excesses were partially limited by the custom of the manors and the charters of the towns.

Medieval society seems static to us who gaze from afar but as Heraclitus said, all things are in flux. Decay rots all society always: it is the pace which varies. The era we conveniently term medieval and feudal was disfigured and brought to an end by the economic consequences of war and pestilence, of baronial faction, of bourgeois strivings, and by the ideas which accompanied the restless Renaissance and the great heresies and schisms of the Reformation.

In the new classical humanism, in the onslaught by men and nations upon the corruption and claims of the Universal Church, and in the rise of the middle class to influence and power, we see the germs of philosophic and political Liberalism. In England a strong central Monarchy rescued the poor and the burghers from general ruin. The boon of peace then seemed inestimable, and it is the measure of public gratitude that a king could replenish his coffers and broaden his support by plundering the monasteries, and that his successors could proceed further and abolish the Mass, all without any widespread revolt.

The trend of the times, then as now, was for the individual to be freed from all restrictions save for those imposed by the central state Leviathan. But things are seldom carried to their conclusion, least of all in England. Englishmen were freed from Rome, but Canterbury and York still stood, and the King became a sort of Pope. The outward form of Church government remained. Canon law still ruled, as did bishops, priests and deacons. The Tudor schools and the Tudor and Stuart Poor Law, so much more enlightened and humane than the Whig measure of 1834, went some way to replace the conventual houses in the scheme of society. The traces of a Catholic order lingered and with it a corporate sense and a feeling for justice between rich and poor.

The Tudors and Stuarts were not afraid to regulate trade in the interest of Crown and people. Catholics like Sir Thomas More, Reformers such as Latimer, Caroline High Churchmen such as Laud, denounced enclosures like the Prophets of old. Laud's Royal master, Charles, endeavoured to regain some portion of the patrimony of the Church, but where Mary failed he could not succeed. The Crown, which sold the booty of the Church to speculating upstarts, was to be humbled by the class which it had ennobled and enriched, and a century after the Bishop of Rome lost his jurisdiction in these islands a saintly monarch lost his head.

With the coming of the Great Rebellion, Whigs and Tories mount the rostrum. But this book is not a history of the Tory Party. Those who want that must turn to Mr. Keith Feiling, to Mr. Maurice Woods and the other authorities on the subject. This is a series of six short biographical studies joined by a common theme of historic principle. The range is from Lord Falkland to Lord Beaconsfield, from the Cavaliers to Tory Democracy. Both Beaconsfield and Falkland are famous men who have been well served by great biographers. No presumptuous attempt is made to improve upon them, and the chapter "Disraeli and After" does not even provide the bare narrative of his life. But who better than that perfect knight Lord Falkland, to give a touch of nobility and ancient virtue to a book of politicians? As for Disraeli, the grandeur of his mind comprehends not only the character and problems of his age but all the centuries before. Today that mind is fresh and relevant. No statesman is more quotable; no statesman of the English past has more to say which can help to revive and save a tired and doubting nation.

The remaining riders in our little pageant are less well known, and less well known than they deserve. Sir Francis Burdett links the Radicalism and the authentic Toryism of

Disraeli's younger days with those disreputable Tories and Jacobites of the eighteenth century. He belongs less to the ranks of the English heroes than to that very English company of notable eccentrics.

Neither William Shippen nor Sir William Wyndham were heroes. Their age was classical, not heroic. The Revolution Settlement in which Rochester, brother to Falkland's friend and biographer, had his secondary part to play, was very much a settlement, and now there must be, "*surtout pas trop de zèle*". Shippen the Jacobite preferred the Senate to the field, debate to conspiracy. Wyndham, who was to lead the "Hanoverian" Tories, took fright before the swords were out.

It seems, therefore, that they were very human, the stuff that political parties are made of: their place in the history of Tory thought and action is impressive and assured.

CHAPTER ONE

Falkland

KING CHARLES THE FIRST lost his head and his Throne. This is well known. Why it happened is the subject of more than one opinion. Some maintain that Charles forced war upon exasperated Parliamentarians only anxious to achieve a balanced constitution and the liberty of the subject. Until the disillusion of 1641 Falkland believed that they entertained "no design against the peace of the kind-dom". But it was as accurate to say that the war was a rebellion made by the moneyed men in order to subject the Crown to the will of an oligarchy. The rebellion was politically possible because King Henry the Eighth's coining of monastic silver, combined with his debasement of the currency and the inflation caused by the influx of American silver, made it more and more difficult for the King to live of his own wealth and rendered him more and more dependent upon the subsidies of Parliament. The sins of the Tudors were visited upon the Stuarts.

It is in the long view irrelevant to debate whether Charles acted arbitrarily. However he acted, whatever his faults as man and Sovereign, the grandees of the new England and the promoters of the Providence Island Company were ultimately bent upon mastery of the State and the Church. They did not want government by King, Lords and Commons, but government of themselves and for themselves. No bishops meant no King.

King Charles's hands were tied by the law; he was *sub lege* as well as *sub Deo*. Divine Right, in Filmer's sense, was not the prevailing theory of the Royalist Party. It is entirely inconsistent with Toryism. Hooker, to whom it owes much, wrote that "by the natural law the lawful power of making laws to command whole politic societies of men, belongeth so properly to the same entire societies, that for any prince or potentate to exercise the same of himself, and not either by express commission immediately and personally received from God or else from authority derived at the first from their consent upon whose persons they impose laws, is no better than mere tyranny".*

For Hooker the seat of law was the bosom of God. In similar fashion Chief Justice Berkeley, when he condemned Hampden, declared that the King's "absolute trust" is to be exerted "according to the laws of the kingdom". The Royal power was more circumscribed than was his vast executive responsibility. "The arms I took up", Charles protested at his illegal and unjust trial, "were only to defend the fundamental laws of the kingdom."

But the Constitution suffered from a lack of definition and of accepted convention, and of this his adversaries took full advantage. The prerogative Courts and the Councils which represented the King's Council on the Marches and in the wilder parts of the King's dominions emanated from the Crown alone. To some they already seemed an unjustifiable anachronism. On the other hand, they had a century's precedent to give them standing, and Common Law was not yet sole and supreme; there was still law merchant, law ecclesiastical and law of State. As agencies of the Royal government, more especially in the period of King Charles's personal rule, that halcyon lull before the storm, the prerogative Courts and the Councils were liked by the common

* *Ecclesiastical Polity*, I, x.

folk, but were odious to the rich men they mulcted for their oppression, men whom the common law often could not touch. Nor did they find favour with the lawyers, a class always prominent in politics, who profited by the common law and its delays. "May the tent of this Court", cried Strafford, "be enlarged, the curtains drawn out, the stakes strengthened, yet no further than shall be a covering to the common tranquillity and shelter to the poor and innocent from the proud and insolent." He meant what he said.

In general, then, the grievances of the Commons' House of Parliament against the Crown and its exercise of the prerogative, were not grievances of the common people. They, for their part, were more concerned with such afflictions as the enclosure of their land, which still went forward apace despite the protests of Churchmen, the Council and the Bench, despite armed riots, the poor man's protest. The grievances of their betters who sat in Parliament were those of men who did very well out of enclosures, as their fathers had supped well on the fat of the Catholic Church. They were sometimes plausible grievances, and they so appear to us who are accustomed to government by King, Lords and Commons, especially the Commons. But "King" Pym and his confederates as opposed to Hyde, Falkland and other constitutional Royalists, were not for the redress of grievances; they did not want satisfaction. As revolutionaries, they depended upon the perpetual agitation of the dissatisfied. They passed legislation for which we are grateful, but they shirked the question of where sovereignty was to reside in the English realm. They declined office under the Crown. They refused to become the King's government like a conscientious opposition whose policy has prevailed. For they, and to a lesser extent the class for which they spoke, coldly determined upon the seizure of power, and if they were not against the monarchy they wished to make monarchy their utensil.

For a time their opposition appeared most loyal, and they carried with them the most conservative of reformers. But by the time Lord Strafford's head was off the issues had become clear to the moderates. Then "began the first breach among themselves, for the Lord Falkland, the Lord Digby and divers other men were for sparing his life, and gratifying the King . . ." "King" Pym was not for gratifying but for humiliating King Charles, and as Strafford had quit his side to become the Monarch's most loyal and most remorseless servant, he had determined not to quit Strafford so long as his head was on.

This Lord Falkland was the second Viscount. His childhood was unhappy, as was that of the King he later served and for whom he died. His father, who had small sympathy for him, was Sir Henry Cary, Baronet, a Gentleman of the Bedchamber and Lord Deputy in Ireland, until recalled in circumstances of some discredit. Young Lucius, small, dark, melancholy of eye and not over-prepossessing, left Ireland with his father. Stripling though he was, the latter had given him a military command. This he now lost, and reading therein an insult to his father and himself he challenged Sir Francis Willoughby, to whom the troops were made over. This temerity landed Lucius in the Fleet prison on a warrant issued by the Privy Council, and he remained there until ten days later when he was released in response to a humble petition preferred by his father.

In Dublin he had studied at Trinity College and was well grounded in Latin and French. During the first part of his residence the Provost was Ussher, later Bishop of Armagh and Primate of all Ireland, but better known to posterity as the originator of a somewhat naïve chronology of the Bible. Ussher was a Calvinist and Lucius was at an impressionable age.

His marriage was happy, and for love. His wife Letice was daughter of Sir Richard Morrison of Tooley Park in the County of Leicester. Letice was poor, and the match infuriated his father. For he did not benefit from the Tanfield property—he had married Elizabeth, daughter of Sir Lawrence Tanfield, Chief Baron of the Exchequer, who had a substantial legal fortune—and Burford Priory and Great Tew descended from Lucius's grandmother, Lady Tanfield, straight to him. She was a great Court lady and Oxfordshire hostess. Impulsive and ever sensitive, Lucius offered his father his grandmother's estate. When it was refused he took himself off to Holland, for the Low Countries were the resort of the bored, the adventurous, and the student of war. His father had soldiered there before him and been taken prisoner by Don Louis de Velasco.

Lucius soon returned to enjoy Great Tew and the arts of peace. He was eager to learn Greek and, being fond of jaunts to London, vowed that he would not go there again until he had mastered it. He read deeply and dreamed much. He was not overfull of vitality but capable of sudden, uncompromising action, capable ever of the unhappiness which assails the intellectual when the times are out of joint. Macaulay wrote that "he was indeed a man of great talents and of great virtues, but we apprehend, infinitely too fastidious for public life", Gardiner that "Falkland was unable to conceive that could be true which was not pure and of good report".

Cary was something of a poet and a keen student of theology, but he lacked real originality of imagination. His main rôle was that of patron. At Great Tew was "one continued *convivium theologicum* or *convivium philosophicum* enlivened and refreshed with all the facetiousness of wit, and good humour, and pleasantness of discourse, which made the gravity of the argument itself delectable". Falkland's friend Hales versified that—

"He was of late so gone with divinity,
That he had almost forgotten his poetry,
Though to say the truth, and Apollo did know it,
He might have been both his priest and his poet."

At Trinity, Dublin, the atmosphere had been favourable to Puritan tendencies. But when Lucius's father died in 1633 after a fall sustained when shooting with the King at Theobalds, he was subjected to the counter-influence of his mother. Lady Falkland had become a Catholic in 1624, and though she carried the zeal of the convert beyond good sense and even charity, she also suffered for the faith. Her husband deserted her and wrote in a letter to Lord Conway of her "serpentine subtlety and that conjoined with Romish hypocrisy". She was constantly harassed and dunned. Lady Falkland declared that her son was "so wholly Catholic in opinion that he would affirm he knew nothing but what the Church told him". Perhaps this was then the case; the mother's persuasions may have proved efficacious, and the young intellect can undergo many transformations. Or again, Lucius may have preferred filial courtesy to an accurate statement of his inner convictions. His subsequent views Lady Falkland put down to his "meeting with a book of Socinus" and to the influence of their mutual friend, William Chillingworth, whom Lucius met at her house. The young lord's relations with his mother were severely bruised when she smuggled two of her other sons to a continental seminary—a deed which brought her to the notice of the Privy Council. Lady Falkland's six daughters, too, were brought up in the old faith; with the exception of the eldest, Lady Home. Financial difficulties also contributed to a temporary estrangement between Lucius and his mother.

But at Great Tew there was friendship and affection. Standing ten miles from Oxford and her University, the place was itself "a University in less volume, whither they came not so much for repose as study". Country houses such as this were centres not only of agrarian sports and duties but also of learned intercourse and, says Aubrey, "the studies in fashion those days in England were poetry, and controversy with the Church of Rome". There foregathered at Great Tew—from London as well as from Oxford—wits, scholars, theologians and poets of the Cavalier school. It was "the first conscious oasis of learning since the break-up of the circle of Sir Thomas More".*

The atmosphere of the place was flavoured with the rich Renaissance mixture of Christian culture with Pagan lore and learning. John Hales, who wrote the verse quoted above, was "one of the least men in the kingdom, and one of the greatest scholars in Europe". Also of the circle were Dr. Gilbert Sheldon of All Souls, who later succeeded Juxon in the See of Canterbury and became a pillar of Royalism and the Establishment, Dr. Earle or Earles who wrote *Micro-cosmographie* and Dr. Morley who, when asked what the Arminians held, replied that they held all the best bishoprics and deaneries in England. Ben Jonson composed an ode to Falkland's passion for Sir Henry Morrison, and John Suckling, careless, cynical—

> "Out upon it, I have loved
> Three whole days together . . ."——

celebrated the coterie in his *Sessions of the Poets*. The host himself rhymed of—

> "Digby, Carew, Killigrew and Maine,
> Godolphin, Waller, that inspired traine."

* David Mathew, *The Age of Charles I.*

"Little Sid" Godolphin and Lord Falkland were "two names of friendship, but one star". There were others, too, like Francis Wenman and Dr. Hammond, and the lord of the house when he came to table did not know who might not be there. This college of Great Tew, "a college situated in purer air", was Liberty Hall for men of wit and learning, not for bumpkins. Falkland loved as much as any squire to dig a fox out with his terriers, but had nothing but pity for "unlearned gentlemen on a rainy day".

Falkland's cicerone in matters theological was William Chillingworth, who epitomized in himself the flux and confusion of contemporary religious strife. A Fellow of Trinity, Oxford, he became a convert to Catholicism under the influence of the Jesuit, Fisher, and lapsed into the Church of England under the influence of Laud, then Bishop of London. He shared with Falkland a latitudinarian desire for religious toleration. Both rested their faith on Reason and the Scriptures. Difficulties over the Thirty-nine Articles and the Athanasian Creed impelled Chillingworth's scrupulous conscience to the refusal of a preferment. He later felt able to accept the chancellorship of a diocese and a prebend, having written in the meantime *The Religion of Protestants, A Safe Way to Salvation*, which achieved great popularity.

Falkland for his part wrote two tracts and a *Discourse on Infallibility*, which was published after his death. For him the Protestant Reformation, itself a rejection of dogma and authority, had no finality and was more to be approved for what it denied than for what it affirmed. He held Anglican dogmatism as noxious as that which the Reformation overthrew, and neither he nor the earnest fraternity at Burford could concede any special sanctity to the age and the findings of the Fathers of the Church. Falkland wanted a church of "volunteers not of pressed men". Righteousness he defined as "seeking the truth impartially, and obeying diligently what is found sincerely". "God will consider the heart rather than the head, the end than the actions, and the fountains than the streams." There was little in common here with William Laud and his ecclesiastical policy. Of the Laudian clergy he remarked that "Common fame is more than ordinarily false if none of them have found a way to reconcile the opinion of Rome with the preferments of England, and to be so absolutely, directly and cordially Papists, that it is all that fifteen hundred pounds a year can do to keep them from confessing it".

He described the aim of the existing bishops as "to try how much of a Papist might be brought in without popery, and to destroy as much as they could of the Gospel without bringing themselves into danger of being destroyed by the Law", and he complained in his speech on the Root and Branch Bill that "while Masses have been said in security, a Conventicle hath been a crime. . . . Some have evidently laboured to bring in an English, though not a Roman, popery. I mean not only the outside and dress of it, but equally absolute, a blind dependence of the people upon the clergy and of the clergy upon themselves: and have opposed popery beyond the seas that they might settle one beyond the water".

Complaints of this kind have been made by Anglicans of the nineteenth and present centuries against Anglo-Catholic tendencies. Resting their case upon the Thirty-nine Articles, they have had greater justification. Falkland in his day was less than just to Laud and his collaborators. As statesman, the Primate was a reactionary; he was bound to Strafford with the strongest bonds of policy and affection. Yet he desired no ecclesiastical tyranny—that was to come from the Puritans—but unity in Jerusalem. He wanted an end to the controversies which, pursued with bitterness and without charity, disturbed the peace of the kingdom. He maintained that God should be worshipped in the beauty of holiness.

The Church of England was fighting for the episcopate and for the Prayer Book—which, more than anything, is the Anglican Church. Ranged against her were what Richard Montague called the Scylla and Charybdis of ancient piety—Papistry and Puritanism. Laud's requirements of dogma and decency of worship would cause small offence in most Low Church parishes of the modern Establishment. " 'Tis superstition nowadays", he complained in 1637, "for any man to come with more reverence into a church, than a tinker and his bitch into an ale-house." In his visitations Laud found parish churches where the misbehaviour of the congregation and the neglect of the incumbent amounted to sacrilege. Communion Tables were used as hat stands and for other profane purposes, cock-fights and betting were known to be conducted in church, and "the vicar of Llanidloes in Montgomery drove the people away from the Holy Communion, refused to use the Prayer Book, received money on the altar, cut the surplices up for use as towels, spoke against the *Book of Sports*, and allowed pigeon-shooting in the church".* If to inveigh against such misconduct was popish, what Anglicans would escape such censure at this present time? The vicar of Llanidloes's condemnation of the *Book of Sports*, which prescribed healthy recreation for after church on Sunday, recalls the Puritan substitution of the Jewish Sabbath for the Christian Sunday, an affliction from which King and Archbishop strove to defend their people.

Despite Falkland's arraignment, Laud's purpose was to tread the *via media* and to preserve traditional religion and the remnants of the old social harmony. He failed

* H. R. Trevor-Roper, *Archbishop Laud.*

and perished on Tower Hill. The sectaries and fanatics triumphed for a space over mirth and art and beauty. Prynne had pointed the way in *The Unloveliness of Lovelocks*, brought out in 1628. "Beautie is no help or furtherance, but a great impediment unto chastitie."

True, the Anglican Church had not been entirely uninfluenced by the Counter-Reformation. Even before Laud became a bishop the general complexion of the Church of England was less Puritanic than it had been under Elizabeth. But though moderate churchmen like Falkland smelled popery, the Laudian divines were not proto-Tractarians. They were more akin, as they were closer in time, to Atterbury and Law than to Pusey or Newman. "A Monarch from his throne", John Keble wrote of King Charles the Martyr, "springs to his Cross and finds his glory there"; but Charles, unlike Keble, never hesitated to call himself a Protestant. He was followed to the wars by Puritan Cavaliers like Sir Jacob Astley, though it may be argued that Astley was prompted by loyalty, not conviction.

Falkland was no Puritan—there was plenty of merry-making at Great Tew—but, as we have seen, he was staunchly Protestant. So were Hyde, Sir Edmund Verney, Digby, Sir John Culpeper. Falkland was not alone in his party in deeming the episcopacy little more than a convenience of church government. Even Lancelot Andrewes, who believed with the judicious Hooker that Law, like the Scriptures, was the voice of God, did not make epicopacy a matter of faith. As an institution, it aroused little enthusiasm. "They who hated the bishops", Falkland said in 1642, "hated them worse than the devil; they who loved them did not love them so well as their dinner." Later he was to become their advocate, and it was of the episcopacy that he uttered the wise maxim: "When it is not necessary to change, it is necessary not to change."

If Lord Falkland was critical of the "Thorough" policy in the Church, he was also no courtier. Flattery, the accomplishment of courtiers, he detested. Yet he was credited with "a great devotion to the King's person". In 1637 he wrote some lines on the occasion of Ben Jonson's death and took the opportunity of congratulating His Majesty upon his assumption of the Sovereignty of the Seas.

Such sovereignty demanded ship money; without it the King's ships could not be maintained nor the coastward towns and villages protected from the raids of Moorish pirates. One estate of Falkland's, not in Oxfordshire, was recorded as in default, but it would be a mistake to suppose that on this question which gave John Hampden so much notoriety Falkland had then decided to oppose the Crown. When, later, he addressed the House of Commons upon Ship Money, it was not so much to condemn the impost as to impugn the conduct of the judges and of Lord Keeper Finch. In 1639 the King, ruling without Parliament and therefore without funds, resorted for the defence of the Scottish Border to the feudal expedient of calling the nobility to arms. Falkland obeyed the royal proclamation, and, disappointed in his hopes of a troop of horse, "went as a volunteer with the Earl of Essex".

For Falkland was a loyalist, though without the passionate devotion of some of the Cavaliers. He had the philosopher's detachment from the sharp divisions of political faction. He had little love either for the Court, despite his kinship with the Hunsdon Careys, or for the opposition, and when the onset of revolution compelled him to take his stand, his tragedy was painfully apparent. He was "fitter", as Clarendon wrote, "to live *in republica Platonis* than *in faece Romuli*", and, like Clarendon, Falkland with his moderation and his scrupulous integrity never gained the intimate confidence of his King. When Secretary of State he went so far as to shrink from the use of informers and the opening of suspect letters.

It was in the Short Parliament that Falkland first appeared in politics and exhibited a reverence for the institution and a belief in its power for good. He had been elected for Newport, in the Isle of Wight, his peerage being of the Kingdom of Scotland, and therefore no bar to membership. He was re-elected to the Long Parliament, when the constituencies went full against the Court, except in Wales, Somerset and some of the loyal northern counties. Pym had conducted an election campaign quite in the modern style, though more corrupt, himself riding about the country and exhorting his countrymen how they should vote.

The Long Parliament ended as an ignoble Rump, and it began its career most infamously with the slow killing of the Earl of Strafford, whom Pym had determined to destroy. It was alleged that "Black Tom" had planned to import an Irish Army to coerce the Commons to their obedience; Pym's real purpose, however, was to forestall him in his intention of boldly impeaching Pym and other ringleaders of the extremist opposition for plotting with the Scots. Therefore, to use Pym's words, "they must not only sweep the house clean below but must pull down all cobwebs".

Sir John Clotworthy, an Ulster settler, Member for Maldon and an adherent of Pym, was put up to report on Strafford's "tyrannical carriage" in Ireland and "the army he had raised there to invade Scotland". The immediate impeachment of the Lord Lieutenant was proposed and a committee of seven set up to consider the impeachment. Pym and Hampden were both members of this committee.

Falkland, making his maiden speech, asked the House not to proceed on imperfect information and undue haste, and suggested that it would "suit better with the gravity of their proceedings first to digest many of those particulars which had been mentioned by a Committee before they sent up to accuse him". He added that "for his own part he was absolutely satisfied that there was enough to charge him". Pym would have none of this. He could not wait for a case to be made out *prima facie*. Strafford was too dangerous to Pym and his party and he must be deprived of his liberty. Told at the Court of Pym's intentions, Strafford fearlessly came down to the House of Lords to confront the worst that his enemies could do. He was called on to withdraw and committed to Black Rod under arrest, and thus the lion was caged.

The blackguard behaviour of the majority in the Commons was partly relieved by the Lords' greater respect for justice. It brought them into ill odour with the Lower House, which was much agitated when Their Lordships granted the Earl of Strafford more time to prepare his defence. Falkland, however, declared that the Peers "had done no more than they conceived to be necessary in justice".

The accused, despite his infirmities and the silencing of his witnesses, defended himself with masterly skill and matchless dignity. The trial having lasted three weeks without a verdict, it became clear to the revolutionaries that Strafford would not be convicted by process of law. They therefore brought in a Bill of Attainder. Lord Digby was assured of Strafford's guilt, and Selden the lawyer had in 1629 been sent to the Tower with Sir John Eliot. Nevertheless, they were outraged by this murderous expedient and opposed the Bill. Falkland spoke in its favour during the debate on the third reading, and it has been asked whether his attitude to Strafford was connected with the latter's treatment of the first Lord Falkland, who had preceded him in the Viceroyalty of Ireland. I think not. Falkland was magnanimous. Moreover, Hyde and Capel were also for the Attainder. The policy of

Thorough in Church and State was repugnant to them all. None, of course, descended to the depths reached by Members like St. John, who considered it unnecessary to discuss the merits and legality of the Attainder; for it was accounted fair play to knock foxes and wolves on the head. Falkland pleaded for mercy for Strafford's family: "They should be spared their estate, for the innocents' sake."

On 8th February, Falkland had attacked the bishops for their conception of Divine Right and for their oppression. He urged the subordination of the clergy to the civil magistracy and the removal of their power of ordering ceremonies "which any member counts unlawful, and no man counts necessary". On the other hand, he considered that the Triennial Act, to which King Charles had assented on the day he agreed to the Bill of Attainder against the Earl of Strafford, would act as a sufficient check upon the bishops. Later, when a bill was introduced to deprive the Lords Spiritual of their seats in the House of Peers, and of their right to hold civil office, Hampden, who had been a welcome guest at Great Tew, gave his personal assurance to Falkland that if it were passed "there would nothing be more attempted to the prejudice of the Church". The bill foundered in the Lords.

In May Falkland spoke against the Root and Branch Bill for the abolition of episcopacy, brought in by Cromwell, namesake and descendant of King Henry's Vicar-General, and the younger Vane. He said it was undesirable and not wanted by the majority, that it was a danger to the cause of learning. In Falkland's mind there was a dread of the Presbyterian tyranny which had already been seen in Scotland. Speaking on the Second Bishops' Exclusion Bill, he rounded on "Honest" John Hampden, who taunted him with changing sides, with the retort that "he had been persuaded by that worthy gentleman to believe many things which he had since found to be untrue and, therefore, he had changed his opinion in many particulars as well as to things superior".

Hyde and Falkland had taken an active and vehement share in the overturning of Strafford and other ministers of the King odious to the Parliament, and in the abolition of such instruments of personal rule as the prerogative courts and the Ship Money tax. They wished the King to govern by and with the advice of Parliament. So ostensibly did Pym and his extremists, but in 1641 their schemes and their more excessive measures were designed to amass all power to the Commons, in anticipation of the slow development of centuries, and that meant to amass all power to themselves.

The murder of Strafford marks the beginnings of the split between Pym's men and the moderate Royalist reformers, but what hastened the formation of a separate party of constitutional Royalists was the attack on the Church of England. Brian Wormald, in his book on Clarendon, argues with conviction that whereas Hyde was chiefly interested in the political implications of episcopacy—if the episcopacy was nothing sacred how should monarchy survive?—Falkland defended Church Order for its own sake. Falkland had attacked the non-spiritual pretensions of bishops, but by the end of 1641 had emerged as the leader of episcopalian opinion. "So long as it was a question of religion as a thing in itself, of its immediate ecclesiastical environment, and of its pure essentials considered apart from politics, of the two, Falkland was pre-eminent in action. But when . . . it became a question of political action which would preserve peace and continuity, ends which were involved in and demanded by religion and the interests of the Church, the parts were reserved and Hyde came to the fore." Between them, Falkland and Hyde gave leadership to a first Tory party of men who stood for the Church, the King and the Laws.

Pym and his party, on the other side, were for a new and radical Reformation. The Grand Remonstrance contained a turgid recital of exaggerated grievances together with a number of revolutionary proposals, including, of course, the exclusion of the bishops from the House of Lords. A synod of divines was to be summoned to settle church matters, and as for the State the King was to be pleased to call to his Council such persons only as were pleasing to Parliament. It is true that bishops were not to be done away with, and Cromwell seems to have imagined that such precocious proposals for the subordinating of the executive to the legislature would command overwhelming approval in the House of Commons. At any rate, he made light of Falkland's plea for more time for debate.

In the event, the discussion of the measure, which began at nine o'clock on a morning in November, 1641, lasted into the small hours of the following day. The debate was attended by tumult and passion. Philip Warwick thought they had all sat in the valley of the shadow of death; "for we, like Joab's and Abner's young men, had catched at each other's locks and sheathed our swords in each other's bowels". The strength of the Opposition to the opposition was shown by the small majority—eleven votes—by which the Remonstrance was passed.

Falkland, who had spoken for the bishops, left the House with Cromwell. He reminded him of their talk about the time given for debate. "Another time", was Cromwell's answer, "I will take your word for it. . . . Had the Remonstrance been rejected I would have sold all I possess next morning and never seen England more, and I know there were many other honest men of the same resolution."

"So near", commented Clarendon, "was the poor kingdom at that time to its deliverance."

On New Year's Day, 1642, the King asked Pym to become Chancellor of the Exchequer. He either ignored the royal summons to an audience or declined to serve. It was the defiance of a revolutionary chief. Next day Culpeper was given the Exchequer and Falkland, persuaded by Hyde, who himself refused a portfolio, became Secretary of State, after long hesitation. As Hyde wrote, "he had not the Court in great reverence and had a presaging spirit that the King would fall into great misfortune; and often said to his friend that he chose to serve the King because honesty obliged him to it; but that he foresaw his own ruin by doing it".

Lord Falkland was governed by principle, not by the passion of loyalty which ruled the hearts of many Cavaliers. One is not surprised to learn that the Secretary quarrelled with Prince Rupert, who, brilliant and versatile, was concerned more with the waging of war than its aims. Falkland's principle was that of moderation and legality in government and of toleration in matters spiritual, and it was a principle no less worthy for its failure to withstand the battering of the revolutionary storm.

In war, as in the opening skirmishes fought in the Long Parliament, Falkland did his duty in obedience to his beliefs. He subscribed to the pacific declaration made by the gathering of Peers at York on the 15th June, 1642, and continued to strive for a peaceful settlement between King and Parliament after the royal standard had been hoisted at Nottingham and blown down with dire ill-omen. It was Falkland who himself carried the second message of Charles to the rebellious Parliament and was directed privately to say that the King would accept a thorough reformation of the Church and other reasonable desires. The offer was rejected, but "when there was any overture or hope of peace he would be more erect and vigorous", for "the view of the calamities and desolation the Kingdom did and must endure, took his sleep from him, and would shortly break his heart". In February, 1643, Falkland was to see the parliamentary commissioners into Oxford, but there was no success in the making of peace. His friend Chillingworth devoted a considerable mechanical talent to the invention of military engines which could bring speedy issue from the conflict. Hyde tells us that he "did really believe all war to be unlawful". Nevertheless, he was captured at Arundel Castle by the Roundheads of Sir William Waller.

At Edgehill the Secretary of State risked his life to save those who had thrown away their arms. The peace-lover did not lack for warlike courage; rather was he "naturally inquisitive after danger". Thus "at the leaguer before Gloucester, when his friends passionately reprehended him for exposing his person unnecessarily to danger . . . he would say merely, 'that his office could not take away the privileges of his age; and that a Secretary in war might be present at the secret of danger', but withal alleged seriously, 'that it concerned him to be more active in enterprises of hazard, than other men, that all might see, that his impatiency for peace proceeded not from pusillanimity or fear to adventure his own person'."

Clarendon noticed that Falkland was always cheerful before action. So it was before Newbury, though he was "weary of the times and foresaw much misery to his country, and did believe he should be out of it by night". He put on a clean shirt, which caused Carlyle to be facetious at the expense of "the little Lord Falkland with his screeching voice but extreme gentility and intellectuality". Before battle he received Holy Communion, and it appears that the charge of Socinianism arose from the importance he attached to Reason as the basis of belief, and that Viscount Falkland died in the Anglican profession.

He attached himself to Lord Byron's regiment and placed himself in the first rank. The regiment advanced upon the Roundheads, who had lined the hedges with musketeers. Falkland rode straight upon a gap and was killed, his body not being recovered till next day, stripped and much mangled. "Thus fell that incomparable young man, in the four and thirtieth year of his life, that the oldest rarely attain to that immense knowledge; and the youngest enter not into the world with more innocence; whosoever leads such a life need not care upon how short warning it be taken from him . . . if there were no other brand upon this odious and accursed civil war, than that single loss, it must be most infamous and execrable to all posterity."

But Clarendon was Falkland's friend, and "in this battle the Chancellor of the Exchequer lost the joy and comfort of his life". Let us rather read the judgment of Whitelocke, the chronicler of Parliament: "His death was much lamented by all that knew him, or heard of him, being a gentleman of great parts, integrity, and honour, courteous and just to all, and a passionate promoter of all endeavours of peace betwixt the King and Parliament."

If much that the Cavaliers believed had descended direct from medieval England, they themselves were in direct lineage from the old orders of chivalry. "A complete cavalier", said Richard Symmonds, "is a child of honour. He is the only reserve of English gentility and ancient valour, and hath rather chosen to bury himself in the tomb of honour than to see that nobility of his nation vassalized."* Lucius Cary differed from the generality of Cavaliers, but he was at one with them in this.

* Keith Feiling, *History of the Tory Party*, 1640-1714.

CHAPTER TWO

Rochester

THE EARL OF STRAFFORD had striven with selfless pertinacity to uphold beyond due time the Elizabethan polity based upon a paternal and popular despotism. It was a system which had enabled England to win glory abroad and to enjoy the more precious gifts of peace at home. It was a species of government which in Strafford's time was proving successful upon the Continent. In courage and ability, in supreme administrative efficiency, in the victories won by a great and generous spirit over fleshly weakness, in the ruthless and untiring pursuit of the policy called "Thorough", Thomas Wentworth, Earl of Strafford, was truly Elizabethan in his magnanimous loyalty. His life and his death were grand. Well might the luckier Richelieu say that "the English were so foolish that they killed their wisest man".

In murdering Strafford the House of Commons removed by judicial injustice the one obstacle in the path of the revolution. To quote the eloquent Sir Philip Warwick, "his station was like those turfs of earth or sea-banks, which, by the storm swept away, left all the inland to be drowned by popular tumult". Yet Strafford hastened the onset of revolt, and history condemns his policy, not because it was not beneficent—the time of his power was a good time for the lowly—but because it did not, and could not, succeed in those disjointed days. The policy of "Thorough" was not conservative; it was reactionary and it was impossible of execution, save at the pike's point, and a régime could not rest on pikes for long. The modern Police State is another story.

The conservative policy of the day was that of the constitutional party which formed about the persons of Hyde and Falkland, his friend, and which combined with loyalty to Crown and Church a zeal for those reforms which the times required. It may have been that a moderating policy was unlikely to channel the revolutionary flood without breaking the dikes of order and peace. It may well have been true that to trust the good intentions of Hampden and Pym was to ride a tiger after its teeth and claws have grown too sharp. But to say that is to be wise after the event; the policy which Hyde and Falkland put forward was a poor best chance of averting the war which threatened.

War finally came because neither King Charles nor the constitutional Royalists could submit to the destruction of their Church. "I tell you", said Charles in his dying speech upon the scaffold of Whitehall, "that I am the martyr of the people." But if he died for the laws and for the poor of the realm he died even more for the cause of the Church of England. He was not only King, he was Governor, and he was more conscious of this ecclesiastical function than was any other Monarch. Charles combined some ineptitude with many Christian virtues. Clarendon, who was not blind in his loyalty, tells us that he "was the worthiest gentleman, the best master, the best friend, the best husband, the best father, and the best Christian, that the age in which he lived produced. And if he were not the best King, if he were without some parts and qualities which have made some Kings great and happy, no other prince was ever unhappy who was possessed of half his virtues and endowments, and so much without any kind of vice". Obstinacy has often been ascribed to the Royal Martyr. Certainly as King, but much more as a Christian of the Anglican persuasion, Charles Stuart was unshakeably determined in the defence of his most cherished principles.

But whether viewed as Christian martyr or as ill-starred despot, Charles the First did not lay his life down in vain. The English never forgot the lesson read them by the experience of a regicide republic. The rebellion which created that republic, whatever the purpose of its unleashing, cut away first the Crown, then the Upper House and finally the Commons' House of Parliament. A rebellion of common lawyers and Parliamentarians was finished by the Generals and the New Model; an Anointed Monarch was succeeded by another single figure, a man of treason, a man whose power exceeded the power not only of Charles but of any Stuart or any Tudor and who, whether he governed through Parliaments or Major-Generals, governed always by *force majeure*.

The subversion of divine monarchy did not do away with the need for a strongly centralized government, and the central power agreeable to English tradition and experience was the power of the Crown. Therefore the Lord Protector was offered the Crown itself, and he refused it not from scruple of political conviction but in submission to the objections of the Army, which was the instrument of his rule. In the future the monarchy which the Cavaliers worshipped and the Tories revered was also to become a necessity to the grandest Whigs who ever compared their lineage and their possessions with those of their Sovereign Lord. The poorer sort were also to learn in sorrow and pain that it was the Crown and the Church which had kept them some measure of justice. The defeat of both in the Civil Wars was the victory not only of lawyers and Parliamentarians and Roundhead generals, of redcoats and black coats; it was also the triumph of competitive economics over social harmony, of trade over tradition, of contract over status, of property over principle. It is of great significance that under the Interregnum the Poor Law was much more harshly administered than by the King in his decade of personal government.

Poor and wealthy alike discovered that if there was insufficient liberty under the King there was none under Cromwell. In religious as in secular affairs the tyranny of the Long Parliament was riveted under the Republic. England must cease to offend Jehovah by deserving the ungodly name of Merry. The great festivals of the Church, even Christmas, were supplanted by strict fasts enforced at the sword's point. It was forbidden to travel by land or by water on a Sunday, except to church, there to hear more from the Old Testament than the New; a man might not walk abroad on the Sabbath with his wife or his sweetheart. Even the Lord's Prayer was prescribed by the devotees of the extempore, but not without resistance. "According to Mrs. Alice Thornton, in one Yorkshire parish the congregation persisted in saying the Lord's Prayer aloud, in spite of the rebukes of the intruding minister; and when he threatened them with eternal damnation for using such a popish invention, an old lady from the pews replied: 'They were no more damned than himself, old hackle-backe'."*

An imposed system of Presbyterianism seasoned with Independent idiosyncracy and Anabaptist licence could not endure. It hardly outlasted Oliver Cromwell. How could it endure? The English were still English. Even Divine Right, whatever it really meant, was patently less overbearing than the rule of saints, sectaries and soldiers. The Presbyterians had not fought for Parliament to allow Protestantism to run amok. They had noted the social peril of movements such

* *Autobiography*, Surtees Society.

as the Levellers and the Diggers. By their invitation, therefore, no less than by that of the old Royalists, King Charles came home to enjoy his own again.

The Restoration was thus not a reaction but a political, social and religious compromise. In future, if the King were to get his way, it would be less by right and power than by the statesman's skill,—of which "the Dark Boy" had plenty—by the manoeuvres and manipulations of party management, the exploitation of personal differences and public passions. Louis XIV's Ambassador reported that "this government has a monarchical appearance because there is a King, but at bottom it is very far from being a monarchy".

The Restoration land settlement, for example, reflected the changes which had occurred and the capitalistic complexion of society. The Church and Crown lands confiscated during the Interregnum were resumed, but those who held them were compensated for their losses by their emancipation from feudal dues, Parliament voting the Excise to the Crown as an equivalent. Estates confiscated because their owners were "Malignants" were given back to their rightful possessors, but no redress was accorded to Royalists who had been forced to sell land to pay the fines imposed by the Long Parliament. The Cavalier Parliament, "a parliament of lewd young men, chosen by a furious people in spite to the Puritans", waxed vitriolic over the land settlement. But they could not prevent many of the results of the Rebellion being preserved in the Restoration.

Clarendon, as Charles's first Lord Chancellor, gave his name to the religious settlement of the Restoration. The Declaration of Breda had promised liberty to tender consciences, but the Clarendon Code was no charter of religious toleration. It did, however, symbolize the failure of an all-embracing Establishment and helped the Dissenting bodies to gain strength through their very disabilities, grievances and sufferings. Had the plan of the Savoy Conference succeeded and Baxter and the Puritan moderates been "comprehended" by the Church of England, the other sects might have languished in isolation. The scheme came to nothing and though Englishmen continued to be reckoned of the Establishment, failing any contrary disposition, the rule of *cujus regio, ejus religio* was now at an end.

Milton had said that a true church may consist of a single individual, and notions of this nature have abounded in the era of plutocratic and bourgeois individualism. The Long Parliament had enforced supposedly Christian rules of morality and conduct by civil authority and had ordained the solemnization of matrimony by Justices of the Peace. Presbyterianism had been established. The trend, however, was not towards a theocracy but towards the separation of State and Church. The Restoration and the Code of Clarendon brought back the Church and its liturgy, but perforce admitted that religious communities might exist within the Nation yet without the National Church. The Catholic tradition of a society corporate in its spiritual as well as its civil aspect lived on in theory and in men's hearts and minds, but would now grow weaker and less real. In ecclesiastical therefore as in political and social matters the Restoration was no recapture of an earlier order of society.

Clarendon held office for only six years after the Restoration. Unlike the French Ambassador, he failed to grasp the underlying significance. Just as Strafford harked back to the previous century, to the Tudor supremacy, Clarendon thought in terms of the fleeting balance of 1640. The executive and the legislative power were becoming mixed together; their battle was done. There would be no more prerogative impositions upon Common Law, though the last conciliar Court, the Council of Wales, endured till 1689. Now, even Cavalier and Tory Parliaments were impelled to invade what was thought of as the sphere of royal prerogative. This Clarendon did not accept, and in 1667 he fell. Cavaliers who had not recovered their lands detested him, and the sale of Dunkirk to the French and our national humiliation by the Dutch in war were outrageous to those we may call Tories and to those we may term Whigs. "... Men spoke of Oliver's day in sorrow, and the guns were heard at London Bridge, there was a run on the banks, placards were posted against Clarendon and 'Dunkirk, Tangier and a barren Queen', there were howls against popery and meetings of the Puritan Lords."* A Country Party arose to oppose that of the Court, combining within its ranks Cromwellians, Presbyterians and Dissenters.

The Cabal followed Clarendon and again defied Tory and national sentiment by the conclusion of the Treaty of Dover in 1670. The object of this Treaty was to give the Crown enough French money to govern without being subjected to the will of Parliament, but the money ran out in 1673. Parliament being re-assembled, Whigs and Tories, if we may use such terms to denote groups of opinion, sentiment and tradition, not organized political parties, united to repeal the King's Declaration of Indulgence which was another means to gaining extra-parliamentary support for personal monarchy. Having passed the Test Act, which made acceptance of the Anglican doctrine of the eucharist and the taking of it according to the Anglican rite a prerequisite to the holding of civil or military office, the Tories again joined with the Whigs to scatter the Cabal and force the ending of the war with the Dutch.

Thus the Tories of the Restoration, like the moderate Cavaliers of Falkland's day, were to be drawn, despite their

* Keith Feiling, *A History of England.*

devotion to monarchy, into recurrent revolt against it. For the sake of independent power the King preferred French money to dependence upon English loyalty. The Declaration of Indulgence was an affront to a Church which was opposed both to popery and to Dissent; the royal foreign policy was the cause of tormenting doubts and self-searching to Royalist squires who presented to their livings parsons such as would preach from the pulpit the doctrine of non-resistance to the Lord's Anointed. It was Charles's fault, not theirs, which impelled these Tories to vote down his policy and to impeach his Ministers. Like Falkland and like Clarendon, when he was plain Edward Hyde and not Lord Chancellor of England, they chose, as men of conscience must always choose, to be more loyal to their Church than to the Crown. They had fought and suffered for them both, but owing to the policy of its wearer it was now less the Crown than the Church which became the symbol of the Tory ideal.

The third Ministry of Charles the Second was headed by Lord Danby, who is regarded as the first of Tory Prime Ministers. Sir Thomas Osborne, Viscount Dunblane, as he then was, was named Lord Treasurer because he could manage the Tory majority in the House of Commons and the country, where he made full use of the various means of royal patronage. He is said to have controlled three hundred and fifty seats through the Lords Lieutenant of Counties. Himself a patriot and anti-French, his service to the Crown involved him in the payment of money from the French King to the English.

It was in vain that Danby implored his Sovereign to exalt his throne by saving Europe from French "thraldom" and planned that Sir William Temple, the admirer of the Prince of Orange who had made the Triple Alliance of 1668 with Holland and Sweden, should become the King's Secretary of State. Charles preferred the safety of neutrality to the hypothetical glories of war. War implied dependence upon the Commons and danger to the prerogative. The Whigs, obsessed by the prospect of a Catholic succession to the English throne, maintained contact with William of Orange, who was therefore a less desirable ally for Charles. The anti-French alliance creaked under constant strain: republican Amsterdam was eager for peace and the Hapsburgs feared a Dutch encroachment upon the Spanish Netherlands.

On the other hand, the national cause held its attractions for Charles the Second. Danby, while further secret treaties were contracted, worked upon his master. Louis was a plain threat to Flanders and therefore to England. A separate peace between France and the Dutch republicans was a dangerous possibility. The King therefore consented to a marriage between the Prince of Orange and his niece Mary Stuart, daughter of James, Duke of York, hoping that this might at once conciliate Parliament and place a restraint upon the ambitions of Louis. The arrangements were made by Sir William Temple. Among the great diplomatist's humbler colleagues in the royal service was Clarendon's second son, the Hon. Laurence Hyde.

Born in the year in which Strafford was impeached, Hyde had sat in the Cavalier Parliament first for the Cornish Newport and then for the University of Oxford. In 1662 he became Master of the Robes and was to remain so for thirteen years. He married a daughter of the first Earl of Burlington in 1665. Both Laurence and his elder brother strenuously defended Clarendon on his impeachment, but Laurence saw little of his father during his seven years of exile. In 1676 he was sent to Vienna to offer condolences to the Emperor Leopold the First on the death of his second consort. Finding, however, that the Emperor had found consolation in another wife, Hyde took up a commission at the instance of Temple to assist as a mediator at the Congress of Nimwegen.

Next year Temple recommended him for a second mission to Nimwegen with special orders to exhort the Prince of Orange to make peace with France. In November the Stadtholder celebrated this marriage with Mary Stuart, he and Charles presented joint terms of peace, and Louis stopped his subsidies to England. Parliament had to be summoned to vote supply and when it met in February, 1678, the Speech from the Throne for once reflected the bellicosity of its Members and their antipathy to Romish France.

The previous month Laurence Hyde had signed a defensive treaty with the Dutch, but his efforts were not followed up by the provision of armed assistance. In the summer, therefore, the French were able to make the Peace of Nimwegen on their own terms, having first isolated the Prince of Orange from the Dutch republican party. Hyde again repaired to The Hague to promise the States-General military aid, but it was too late. Temple, who had not been consulted, described Hyde as much mortified by "the entire disappearance of the design upon which he came, and believed the Court passionately bent".

All Danby's efforts ended in failure for his policies and ruin for himself. Like the Parliamentarians under Charles the First, the Whigs demanded a forward policy on the Continent of Europe but denied the Crown the means to pursue it. They agitated for the disbandment of an army which might be used to strengthen the Monarchy at home. Fervent Protestants, they took French money to buy the votes of the electors, and it was the French who disclosed to them a letter betrayed by Montagu, lately our ambassador in Paris, which revealed Danby's share in the negotiations for Louis's subsidies to Charles. A proper scepticism when the "Popish Plot" was revealed to a receptive nation also helped to encompass the destruction of Danby.

Covenanting preachers had appeared in England as if from nowhere. Armed and martial, they rode the length and breadth of the kingdom ranting a militant Protestant message. The summer of 1678 was hot, the air heavy with rumour and fear. Not a century had passed since the Gunpowder Treason. Every year it was noisily commemorated. The Queen and the heir apparent were Papists. Jesuit emissaries crossed and recrossed the water. In the Chapel of the Savoy the incense smoked and the Romish Mass was celebrated. If poor men had ancestral memories of rack and stake, there were rich men who might quake for their abbey lands. To a country in such case Israel Tongue and the perverted renegade Titus Oates unloosed the murderous fabrication of the Popish Plot. To their greed for power and fame were sacrificed the lives of innocents and the honour of England. The King and his judges quailed impotently before the fury of the mob. "Let the blood lie on them that condemn them," said the Monarch, with the death warrants before him, "for God knows I sign with tears in my eyes."

To doubt the Plot meant denunciation and arrest. Panicky citizens carried for their protection a weapon called "the Protestant Flail". Delation flourished. Deane and Pepys, saviours of the Royal Navy, went to the Tower. A new Parliament met in March, 1679. Hyde was Member for Wootton Bassett. For the most part it was packed with Presbyterians and Independent and Republican adherents of the Good Old Cause. Danby, vainly hoping that his adversaries might be appeased by the removal of the Duke of York from the kingdom, was swept away. The King could not save him. Nor could he save loyal Catholic subjects from the gallows and its shambles. All he could do was to wait for the fire to burn itself out.

That it should not burn out was the malignant purpose of Lord Shaftesbury, "restless, unfixed in principles and place". Sir John Cooper's son, Anthony Ashley, had sat in Parliament with Falkland, and had been the King's man till the Civil War was on and he was deprived of the governorship of Weymouth. He turned his coat and became a member of the Lord Protector's Council of State, only to part company with Cromwell also. Sir Anthony was among the commissioners appointed to draw up the invitation to King Charles the Second to enter into his kingdom, and was given a barony and other honours at the joyous Restoration. Until 1667 he remained with the Court Party, but resisted the religious settlement. After the fall of Clarendon, he was numbered of the Cabal and became Lord Chancellor and Earl of Shaftesbury. With the withdrawal of the Declaration of Indulgence and the Treaty of Dover, Shaftesbury severed his association with the Court to become the presiding genius of the Country Party.

After Danby's degradation Charles proceeded to a reorganization of his Privy Council based in great part upon recommendations made by Sir William Temple. It was reduced in size and was to consist half of ministers and half of other notables. Charles's intention, which was not fulfilled, was to dispense with any kind of inner council or cabinet. Monmouth and the Opposition leaders were included. The Earl of Shaftesbury became Lord President, but was dismissed from office after a few months. The attempt to govern on inter-party lines proved a failure and a council was once again formed within the Council. Parliament was dismissed in July. "I will submit to anything", the King said, "rather than endure the House of Commons any longer."

The principal Ministers under the new dispensation were Robert Spencer, second Earl of Sunderland, Sidney Godolphin and Laurence Hyde, who was named a Lord of the Treasury when it was put into commission on Danby's downfall. Being young, they were laughed at as "the Chits".

> "But Sunderland, Godolphin, Lory,
> They'll appear such chits in story,
> 'Twill turn all politics to jests,
> To be repeated like John Dory,
> When fiddlers sing at feasts."

But they were conscientious and industrious in the public service. Of the three, Hyde, who became First Lord of the Treasury, alone held abiding principles. These were the Cavalier and Tory principles of Church and King. An able courtier and a defender of prerogative, Laurence Hyde was steadfast against Rome, but had the confidence of York, who had married his sister Anne. He tried without success to bring an Anglican priest to her death-bed in March, 1671. He ever longed for James's reconversion, and in this hope travelled to Scotland to see him early in 1681.

Shaftesbury and the Country Party continued to inflame the passions evoked by the popish scare. Monmouth, a bastard but a Protestant, toured as on a royal progress, exhibited his charms, touched for the evil and ran races with the rustics. It was spread about that the King had really married his mother, Lucy Walters. Shaftesbury was adept at arousing the *mobile vulgus* and had a flair for party management. Beer and bribes were used to the utmost, parliamentary candidates were coached in party policy, and political dinners were held when Parliament was sitting. Himself an atheist, Shaftesbury headed the demand for the cutting of the Duke of York from the succession to the throne of his brother and the securing of the Protestant succession through the Duke of Monmouth. For, said his confederate Lord Russell, King James's subjects would either burn or become Papists. Shaftesbury's physician and confidant was the philosopher John Locke, to whom Liberal political theory owed much and who had already formulated his ideas upon the relations of Church and State.

By such means as a scurrilous press and the Green Ribbon Club, in Fleet Street, which swayed the City of London with its Civil War tradition of insurgent trainbands, Shaftesbury promoted petitions for an early meeting of Parliament. When Parliament was not sitting his capacity for mischief was confined and his influence of small avail. The Court Party replied with counter-petitions opposing the demand for the calling of Parliament. It was thus and then that the two parties became known as "Petitioners" and "Abhorrers" or "Whigs" and "Tories". Tories were popish Irish bandits and Whigamores Scotch Covenanters. In the vivid language of the Reverend Titus Oates, "these then for their Eminent Preying upon their Country, and their Cruel, Bloody Disposition, began to show themselves so like the Irish Thieves and Murtherers aforesaid, that they quickly got the name of Tories".*

Parliament at length met in October, 1680. The Commons carried the Exclusion. Sidney Godolphin opposed the Bill, and reference was made to the loyalty of the early Christians to the Apostate Julian and to the Romish origin of the principle of deposition. The Lords threw it out on first reading by sixty-three votes to thirty. The credit is due to George Savile, Earl of Halifax, who had been accounted a Whig but disliked and despised party faction and believed in hereditary monarchy. Sunderland, then a Protestant, supported Exclusion. Hyde, although he admitted that it might be necessary to limit by statute the powers of a Roman Catholic king, impugned the injustice of the Bill. "He was concern'd for the honour of the House's equity, not to condemn a person without hearing him or any process

* Jane Lane, *Titus Oates*.

against him." During its discussion in the Commons it was pointed out that the Bill was consistent neither with hereditary monarchy nor with the oath which Members took to the King, his heirs and successors. A majority had been secured, however, for Exclusion, thanks to the popish scare, the electoral efficiency of Shaftesbury and the genuine national dread of a persecuting prince. They refused to vote supply until the Exclusion Bill was passed, and Charles dissolved his Parliament in January, 1681.

A new Parliament was summoned in March to loyalist Oxford. The King's Horse Guards lined the Windsor road; Oxford was like an armed camp. The London members came with ribbons in their hats bearing the motto of "No Popery, No Slavery". Shaftesbury insisted that Monmouth be recognized as heir to the throne. He refused a royal offer that James should be banished and the Prince of Orange act as his regent, and the Oxford Parliament lasted a week. Shaftesbury's adherence to Monmouth while other Whigs supported William of Orange weakened his position and that of his party, and his very violence told against him. The dissolution of King Charles's last Parliament, that of Oxford, marks the beginning of a Royalist revival.

The King was now thrown back on financial assistance from France. Hyde, who in April, 1681, became Viscount Hyde of Kenilworth, was caught up, like Danby, in Charles's secret and anachronistic diplomacy which, by helping the aggrandizement of Louis XIV, ran counter to British sentiment and security. From his personal point of view, an anti-French policy would have meant the supremacy of Halifax and the calling of Parliament, and the calling of Parliament meant that the legitimate succession would be in jeopardy. Hyde, moreover, owed much to the favour of the Duke of York. So it was that at a time when the Prince of Orange was writing that "it is only by you in England that the Netherlands can be saved", Hyde was negotiating with Barillon for a secret subsidy for Charles. In so doing he denied the interests of his country that he might save the succession—and himself, but the choice was of two evils. The negotiations achieved their object, and he whom Evelyn styled the "great favourite" rose higher in the King's opinion. In November, 1681, Hyde became Earl of Rochester, a new creation, not to be confounded with the title held by the somewhat prurient poet, John Wilmot.

With the dissolution of Parliament, Charles, whose statesmanship was of the most acute, fully profited from the errors and disunity of the Country faction and from the general sentiments of shame at the cruelties lately practised upon the Catholics. The Tories for their part had learned the mechanics of party political organization. They started a party press, and adopted party candidates, who wore little red ribbons in their hats. True blue was then a Whig colour. A Loyal Society was founded, and at Oxford University the undergraduates displayed their devotion when welcoming the King by forcing the passers-by "to carouse on their knees a health to their beloved Charles".* The Duke of York and Albany became for a while "the glory of the British line".

Strengthened by a new outpouring of devoted loyalty, by the scotching of conspiracies which gave fresh impulse to that loyalty, the confiscation of charters—Judge Jeffreys on the Northern Circuit "made all the charters, like the walls of Jericho, fall down before him"—and the remodelling of corporations for the sake of a Tory majority, and financed by the £200,000 which Rochester had arranged for him, "Old Rowley" governed to the end without Parliament in despite of the Triennial Act of 1664. Now the axe of persecution was turned towards the Whigs. Shaftesbury was

* Anthony Wood, quot. Keith Feiling, *The History of the Tory Party, 1660-1774*.

accused, later escaping to Holland. Dryden published his *Absalom and Achitophel* to rouse his readers against him. Monmouth, like Shaftesbury, took refuge in the Low Countries.

The Merry Monarch's star was in the ascendant, though the light was soon to be put out by death. Rochester's fortunes did not keep pace with his master's. He was untractable and overbearing in success, and always quick to anger, particularly when in his cups. "His infirmities," wrote Roger North, "were passion, in which he would swear like a cutter, and the indulging himself in wine". Jeffreys was later a fellow-toper, for he suffered grievously from the stone. The story goes that the Lord Chancellor and the Lord Treasurer (as Rochester became under King James) were at a dinner given by a rich alderman to members of the Government, and grew so drunk that they stripped themselves all but stark and were with difficulty restrained from climbing a signpost to drink a loyal toast. Nor did Rochester possess the art of dissimulation essential to the courtier who would survive. Sunderland combined against him with Godolphin and the Duchess of Portsmouth, mistress of His Majesty. In Halifax, Rochester had a rival of parts.

Already disappointed of the Lord Treasurership, Rochester was in August, 1684, "kicked upstairs" from the Treasury Board to the Presidency of the Council. The phrase was Halifax's. "I have seen people", he said, "kicked downstairs, but my Lord Rochester is the first person I ever saw kicked upstairs." In October, he was appointed to succeed the Duke of Ormonde at Dublin, but never left for Ireland owing to the death of his daughter, Lady Ossory, and instead retired into privacy. It was noticed that this retirement coincided with the opening of an investigation, proposed by Rochester, into certain treasury books for which he was accountable. Halifax charged certain contractors with fraud and corruption; Rochester took the matter as a reflection upon his integrity and honour. It was whispered that the Earl would soon be in the Tower. The King determined to annul the offending contract. Before he could do so, he was dead of a sudden stroke, but not before Father Huddleston, who had risked his life for him during the escape from Worcester field, had administered the last rites of the Catholic Church.

When James came to the throne the loyalist tide had not begun to recede. This does not mean that the accession of a Roman Catholic left the minds even of Tories entirely undisturbed. They detested Shaftesbury, his views and works, but, unlike that atheist, were devoted to the Reformed Establishment. They greeted the accession with hope, but few were entirely unprepared for disappointment.

The hostile influence of Rochester's enemy, her Grace of Portsmouth, died with her lover, and it was not long before King James made his brother-in-law Lord High Treasurer and a Knight of the Garter. Rochester had the confidence of the Catholic King, but this is no way lessened his attachment to the Church of England. At Easter James decided to celebrate the day with a procession to and from his chapel. For the first time for a century and a quarter the Roman Mass was to be celebrated at Westminster. Not only the Household but the Ministers of State should take part. Rochester refused to join in without a definite and precise command from the King, and James, respecting his conviction, permitted him to withdraw to the country for Easter. The other Ministers attended, false Sunderland, who was continued as Secretary, with opportunist alacrity. The Guards paraded. The Duke of Somerset carried the Sword of State. Ormonde and Halifax remained in the antechapel. Only Rochester stayed away.

James's treatment of his Minister's susceptibilities was a mark of special esteem. Tact and flexibility were not often exhibited by the Monarch of whose *sottise* his predecessor was wont to speak. But Rochester had to share his favours with Sunderland, who was not handicapped by religious scruple, and was soon to outstrip him. Halifax, however, gave way as Lord Privy Seal to Rochester's elder brother, Henry, Earl of Clarendon, also a staunch Anglican and Royalist. It was the Trimmer's turn to be kicked upstairs.

Sunderland organized the Tory victory in the General Election which followed the demise of the Crown. Slogans of the day were "No Black Box",—Shaftesbury had claimed secret information of the legitimacy of Monmouth—"No Bill of Exclusion" and "No Association", that being the Exclusionist organization. Charles's remodelling of corporations contributed to the success of the counties; even Cheshire, Monmouth's stronghold, fell to the Monarchy. In a House of Commons of three hundred and fifty James could depend on all but forty; Argyll's rising against him was crushed and the rebellion of Monmouth was not supported by the Whigs except in the Roundhead West. The simple, unhappy army of the Protestant hero was routed among the "rhines" of Sedgemoor, and Monmouth in bonds pleaded ignominiously for life. He begged Rochester to intercede for the King's clemency, but the royal bowels of mercy were closed against him, and he passed to his bungled execution.

The Catholic King was now firmly seated upon the throne and a policy of magnanimity and moderation might have enthroned him also in the hearts of a Protestant nation. Instead, he planned to exploit Rochester and every faithful servant to assault the liberties of the Church for which his father had died and to which his most loyal subjects were devoted. To stamp upon the affections of the Tories in the hope of propping himself upon the Catholics and Dissenters he proposed to indulge was to cut the ground from beneath the throne. But this was what he did. "I shall make it my endeavour", he told his delighted Council upon succeeding his brother, "to preserve this Government, both in Church and State, as it is now by law established. I know the principles of the Church of England are for Monarchy, and the members of it have showed themselves good and loyal subjects; therefore I shall always take care to defend and support it." Rochester asked that the declaration be signed and published, and this was done. It could scarcely have been possible for the King to state more clearly the opposite of what he tried to do.

Rochester protested after Sedgemoor that no more Papist officers should be commissioned. In November, 1685, both Houses of Parliament attacked the royal claim to use the dispensing power and the illegal appointment of Catholic officers. A Tory House of Commons resolved by a majority of one to withhold supply until grievances were redressed. Parliament was therefore prorogued and not summoned again by King James. Then were sown the seeds of estrangement between the Tories and Anglicans and the Crown.

Rochester's position became less secure. Unlike Sunderland, he could not accommodate himself to men like Father Petre, who exercised immense if unostentatious influence upon the King, and was even admitted to the Privy Council in 1687. Sunderland, who became a convert, urged the King forward along the road of madness. Some thought that he designed to destroy his master. It must not be supposed that the policy of Romanization roused the enthusiasm of the Catholic nobility and gentry, a breed which had lavished blood and treasure upon the first Charles and now, though legally debarred from the magistracy and office, lived in amity with their Tory neighbours. Rochester had the support of the papal nuncio and the Spanish ambassador Ronquillo. Petre's Jesuit group was for France; Sunderland became a pensioner of the *Roi Soleil.* The Pope himself and Mansuete, who was the King's confessor before Petre, advised moderation. But James was incapable of that.

In the hope of averting his own downfall, Rochester allowed himself to be appointed to the Court of Ecclesiastical Commission. This was the name under which the King revived the High Commission, abolished by the Long Parliament with the approval of Falkland and Hyde, in order to manage the Church of which he was not a practising member and to impose his creatures upon the Universities. Clarendon implored Rochester "not to hurt the best Church in the world". Rochester had no intention of so doing, and he was not long to have the power. Indeed, Burnet says that Rochester told him that after the Monmouth rebellion he was never consulted by the King save on treasury business.

Instigated by Sunderland, James bade Rochester be instructed in the Catholic faith. He at length agreed to hear it stated in the presence of two Anglican clergymen, but himself treated the display with haughty indifference. It was apparent that James's favours were coming to an end. Mary of Modena blamed him for the ascendancy of Catherine Sedley, also known as Countess of Dorchester, in the affairs of the King's heart. It was believed that Rochester was using this lady, whose Protestantism was more apparent than her morals, to woo the King back to a policy of restraint. Sunderland and Father Petre declared that Rochester must go if the Test Act were to be repealed. The King wept at a last interview in December, 1686; in January, the Treasurer's white staff was surrendered. Clarendon, recalled from Ireland where he had been Deputy, had already written to his brother that he blessed God "for the grace and courage He has given you to persevere in the right, and to tread the steps my father went before us". It was not much later that Rochester lost the Wardrobe also amid a general clearance of Tory worthies. Barillon spoke of the triumph of the "Catholic cabal"—a small group to be distinguished from the Catholic lords and gentlemen who were opposed to the insensate bigotry of James and whom the French Ambassador contemptuously dubbed "*les bons Anglais*".

James admitted in Council that there was no question of "dissatisfaction" with Rochester. He kept early hours at the Treasury and worked industriously. But there was no question either of his re-appointment to the new Commission, which was manned by two Catholic and three other Lords, of whom Lord Godolphin was the most competent. Rochester received no office, except the Lord Lieutenancy of Hertfordshire, which he loyally strove to turn to the royal profit. As for Henry, Earl of Clarendon, he was superseded by the Catholic Tyrconnel. The Hydes were in eclipse. In justice to James, it must be mentioned that he provided Rochester with a handsome living from the revenues of the Post Office.

In the two years remaining to him James, with ready use of prerogative and dispensing power, rushed headlong upon revolution. In the course of one short disastrous reign the doctrine of non-resistance and the theory of Right Divine—Filmer's *Patriarcha*, which was published in 1680, was a Tory text-book until the Revolution—were clearly seen to be incompatible with Tory faith and Tory patriotism. The Glorious Revolution, though almost bloodless, was not really glorious; it was a tragic necessity imposed by a King who flouted reason and the loyalty of the loyal, and so destroyed the dynasty. We speak of the Whig Revolution, but without the Tories it would never have been carried through.

William, with commendable timing, landed at Torbay on Guy Fawkes' Day. James was about to set out for his camp at Salisbury, when Rochester, together with his old opponent Halifax, proposed and set his hand to a petition for a free Parliament and negotiations with the Dutchman. Among the other signatories were Clarendon, Rochester's father-in-law, Lord Burlington, and five bishops of the Establishment. They wanted not the deposition or the abdication of James, but rather that the laws of England should not be changed.

On his return from Wiltshire James called a meeting of forty or fifty peers, spiritual and temporal, who were in or near the capital, to discuss the summoning of Parliament. They met at the Guildhall in December. Rochester and those of like mind again set themselves to the toil of saving their Sovereign from himself, though Clarendon spoke with impolitic bitterness. Lord Dartmouth, who commanded the royal fleet, was directed to disarm his Catholic officers—Rochester later also signed the peers' order to restrain the fleet from resistance—and a declaration to the Prince was drafted and signed by Rochester, Viscount Weymouth and the Bishops of Rochester and Ely. This document thanked the Prince for coming to save the kingdom "from the imminent dangers of Popery and Slavery" and undertook that the signatories would help him to call a free Parliament, "wherein our laws, our liberties, and properties may be secured, the Church of England in particular, with a due liberty to Protestant Dissenters". English support for the Protestant war was also promised. The need for English arms and resources decided the Stadtholder's consent to intervene.

The most loyal attempts at a settlement were, however, ineffective. James was determined upon flight to France and was confirmed in this purpose by his Queen. Agreement with Orange would have meant the sacrifice of the priestly clique which imposed upon James without having the support of the English Catholics or of the Holy See and now worked upon the feelings and the ignorance of Mary of Modena. Here lay the answer to Rochester's agonized question, "O God, what could make our master desert his kingdoms and his friends?" Brought back from a first attempt and warmly received by the common people, James eventually departed for France—escape is not the word, for William wanted him gone. With him departed the prime Tory objection to the recognition of the Prince. As Rochester said, "What can the most loyal and dutiful body in the world do without a head?" And to Northumberland, when the news reached them of King James's flight: "Muster your troop of Guards, and declare for the Prince of Orange."

The Tories were dismayed by their success at revolution. For the Whigs, the party of Exclusion, a deposition presented fewer problems. For them a contract had been dissolved and a new one was to be drawn. But in the inmost being of the Tories, bridling at the Dutch bluecoats mounting guard at St. James's, the instinct for legitimacy survived the failure of Divine Right. At first they would not admit that the throne was vacant; indeed to do so would amount to approving the succession of James the Third, of whom there were many doubts. Danby believed him illegitimate and proposed that Mary was lawful Queen and William her Prince Consort. Rochester was among those who backed the project for a Regency advocated by the gentle Archbishop Sancroft and supported by the Church. Failing a Regency, Princess Mary should be made Queen. The project miscarried: it was unacceptable both to William and to Mary. Rochester lost the new Queen's favour for a while, despite their common attachment to the Anglican Church.

Rochester accepted the accomplished fact and in March, 1689, took the oath which was rejected by that distinguished and admirable section of the Anglican bishops and clergy who put allegiance before livings and became the non-juring church. They were a distinguished and honourable body. Besides Sancroft, they included the Bishops of Bath and Wells, Peterborough, Chichester, Ely, Gloucester, Worcester and Norwich. Some of their number returned later to the parent body. But the non-juring community continued to exist with gradually diminishing numbers until well on into the nineteenth century. In matters of liturgy they had a freer hand than the State Church, and their revision of the Communion office was influenced by ancient tradition and the Orthodox rite. Macaulay had no use for their unflinching consistency. Their sacrifice, which is undoubted, was for him a sacrifice of "both law and order to a superstition as degrading as the Egyptian worship of cats and onions". Such cynicism is unworthy of the great Liberal historian.

Gilbert Burnet, whom William had made Bishop of Salisbury, asked Rochester to mediate with the Non-Jurors. An Episcopalian Scot, he worked for understanding between his own Communion and the prevailing Presbyterian Church. The first two volumes of his *History of the Reformation* which appeared in the reign of Charles the Second earned him the thanks of Parliament. The offer which Rochester was authorized to convey was that Sancroft and his brethren might be excused taking the oath if they would continue to perform their spiritual duties. The proposal appeared liberal; but it was altogether unacceptable, for the Anglican liturgy includes regular prayers for the King and Queen by name. The Non-Jurors promised, however, to live peaceably, and they kept their word.

By refusing to interfere in the trouble which arose between the Queen and Princess Anne over the Marlboroughs' dismissal, Rochester regained Mary's goodwill. In 1692 he was re-admitted to the Privy Council. Rochester, Seymour, Danby and Daniel Finch, second Earl of Nottingham, ranked among the King's firmest supporters, and they were all Tories; Nottingham was even exempted from King James's promise of pardon. Both he and Rochester were among the opponents of the Place Bill of 1692, which was intended to remove the royal power of patronage, and was rejected by the narrowest of majorities. It had been better if at that time the party who claimed support from the people rather than from plutocracy had called for a thorough reform of the representative system. But politicians are not always wise and seldom prescient.

In February, 1696, the King told Parliament of the uncovering of a plot to murder him on the return from hunting in Richmond Park. Seizing their opportunity, the Whigs demanded an "association", declaring William "the rightful and lawful King of these realms", and vowing to wreak vengeance, should he be assassinated. The House ordered that all should subscribe this oath next day. Nottingham and Rochester put forward their concept of *de facto* monarchy, the latter with the utmost vehemence. It was an ugly situation. The Tory peers were eventually mollified by an adroit formulation by Danby, now Duke of Leeds. William, instead of being admitted "right and lawful" King, should be deemed to have "the right by law".

The Assassination Plot was succeeded by proscription and persecution. Sir John Fenwick, a most outspoken Jacobite, was implicated, but the Whigs were unable to get him convicted in the courts, so in the Pym tradition brought in a Bill of Attainder. Rochester spoke and signed a protest against this act of blood, and was supported in his stand not only by the Tories but by moderate Whigs and even placemen besides. Such men held that it were better to leave Fenwick unpunished than to make a law for punishing him.

Rochester's fortunes revived when the Whig Junta was forced from office. This happened as the result of the King's disposal, without the parliamentary approval he had agreed to obtain, of Irish lands forfeited in the war against him. The Commons' enquiry reported that a million acres had been divided between the Dutch favourites, Joost van Keppel, Earl of Albemarle, and Hans Willem Bentinck, Earl of Portland. Rochester became Lord Lieutenant of Ireland and virtually First Minister, with Robert Harley to manage the Commons. In the ensuing General Election of December, 1700-January, 1701, the Tory Country Party swept the polls. By the end of the reign they were seated firmly in the saddle.

William described the imperious and irascible Rochester's term of office as "one of the uneasiest of his whole life". He was seldom in Ireland and made little impression upon the administration of that unfortunate kingdom, but Burnet says that Rochester had so much the confidence of the Establishment that he was able to tolerate Irish "Dissenters as well as Papists". Early in 1702 William told Rochester that he purposed to relieve him of the Lieutenancy, but he died as opportunely as Charles the Second, and Anne confirmed her uncle in office and made one of his daughters a Lady of the Bedchamber.

In Anne the Tories could bow the knee to a Queen who was at once a fervid Anglican and a Stuart, and under her the Church attained the summits of power and popular esteem. Dr. Sacheverell denounced comprehension of Dissenters and preached the dependence of government upon religion. "Let us steadily adhere", he wrote in his Discourse on that subject, "to the old staunch principles of our Church."

The Parliament of 1702-5 was a Tory Parliament; the Queen's Ministry was at first a restless Coalition. The exigencies of the War of Spanish Succession had the effect, however, of elevating Marlborough and Godolphin.

Rochester, and Nottingham by his side, were typically Tory in their dislike for the blood and frustration of long campaigns upon the Continent. The sinews of war was the tax upon land. The High Tories held that England should play a secondary rôle in that theatre of war. The controversy recalls those which raged in later days when other despots warred against the liberty of European nations and the security of Great Britain. If England must fight, argued Rochester, let her fight upon the seas where she is sovereign. Let her mariners grapple with Spain, despoil her colonies, destroy her shipping, cripple her commerce. Let England hold the Mediterranean gate—the gate to the Eastern trade.

Marlborough, whatever his political wanderings, crowned the Whig ascendancy with laurel. The march to the Rhine and the victory of Blenheim were glory to England, but repugnant to Tory war policy. Peterborough became the symbol of that. Charles Mordaunt, Earl of Peterborough and Monmouth (of the second creation), was a general and a politician of turbulence and fury. Macaulay said that he was the last of the knight-errants. He had advocated Triennial Parliaments against the wishes of King William. In 1697 he had been implicated in the bloody affair of Fenwick, had been consigned to the Tower and suffered the striking of his name from the council book. As commander in Spain he achieved signal successes, but was recalled in 1707 with insult and ignominy. Rochester, supported by Lords Nottingham and Haversham, extolled his services and moved a vote of thanks. The Queen was privately present at the debate. They proposed that the Spanish front be reinforced at the expense of Marlborough.

But we are too far forward in the narrative of Rochester's life. While Marlborough saved Holland from Louis the Tories raged, not without reason, at the scandal of

Occasional Conformity, under which Dissenters profaned the sacrament for the sake of office. Meanwhile Godolphin, the able Treasurer, and Marlborough, the soldier of genius, attained effective control of the Queen's Government. Rochester was clearly out of place. Always likely to be "a difficult and prickly man", he freely criticized his colleagues, Godolphin in particular, and it was found intolerable that he uttered in debate secrets learned in cabinet. In 1703 the break came. At Marlborough's instance, the Queen ordered Rochester to his Irish charge. When a week passed and he was still this side of the Irish Sea, his resignation was compelled, and the second Duke of Ormonde succeeded to the Lord Lieutenancy.

Lord Nottingham ceased to be Secretary of State, and there came in with Harley and St. John a less inveterate school of Toryism. Robert Harley was brought up a Puritan. Henry St. John was in his earlier years red-hot, but it was Lord Bolingbroke who was to dispose of the corpse of Divine Right and to re-chart the Tory course.

It was not long before Harley and St. John went the way of "the wild faction" of Nottingham and Rochester. "Wild" they appeared to moderates like Harley; but Rochester himself never strayed upon the Jacobite by-road. That course suffered from the unstable support of the French King. The cause slipped back when Louis recognized the Old Pretender as James the Third. In 1692 the naval victory of La Hogue was greeted with national rejoicing. Whigs and Tories gave thanks to God. Sidney and Portland went to Portsmouth to greet and congratulate the victorious fleet, and Rochester went with them as representative of the Tories. It was the same in 1708, when the news that the Pretender had put out from Dunkirk in French bottoms and appeared off the Firth of Forth was received with a similar surge of national feeling.

Rochester's cardinal allegiance was to the Anglican Church. He was unyielding and intolerant in his loyalty. His firm resistance to James the Second's attempt to convert him by priestly instruction to the older religion of England strengthened many feeble knees among the Protestant loyalists. It was on ecclesiastical grounds that Rochester opposed the Regency Bill, designed to smooth the Protestant succession on the death of Queen Anne. Staunch Anglicanism also prompted Rochester's opposition to the Union with Scotland, which was carried through in 1707. The position of the Church of Scotland was guaranteed, and (most horrible!) Presbyterians would take their seats at Westminster.

Rochester doubtless remembered then that the Scots had burnt him in effigy at Edinburgh in 1695. It was the year in which William Paterson, the Scots founder of the Bank of England, started a project for a trading settlement on the Isthmus of Darien which would sit astride the western and the eastern trade and "wrest the keys of the world from Spain". William the Third disliked the scheme, whether on account of Dutch mercantile interests or no. He did nothing to rescue the Scottish colonists of New Caledonia from the ensuing fury of the Dons. Rochester had said that "if these Scots are to have their way, I shall go to settle in Scotland, and not stay here to be made a beggar".

The Whig domination of 1708 ended in 1710. The Tories wanted an end of the war, whose expense was ruinous. As Swift wrote in *The Conduct of the Allies*, "The High Allies have been the ruin of us. We are paying the Allies to be allowed to fight their battles for them". The cost of the war helped to do for the Whigs, who had set their faces against any peace which did not restore to the House of Austria the whole monarchy of Spain. So did the overreaching ambition of the Duke of Marlborough to be made Captain-General for life. So did the unwise impeachment of Dr. Sacheverell, the champion of High Church. A Tory Ministry was installed in 1710 and a Tory majority took their seats in the House of Commons. Harley became Chancellor of the Exchequer and was invested next year with the office of Lord High Treasurer and raised to the peerage as Earl of Oxford. Rochester, now aged and ailing, became President of the Council, and held that office until his death in 1711.

Late in the day he calmed his enthusiasms. The Electress Sophia, who had been named as Anne's successor in the Act of Settlement, thought well of him, and in his last month on earth he was opposing the dismissal of Marlborough. The thread of consistency running through his career was his unswerving fidelity to the Anglican cause, and this was the hallmark of the Tory of his day. The choice between a Protestant Hanoverian and a Catholic Stuart might bedevil the unity of the Tory groupings, but with the Throne in doubt all was made to rest upon the Altar.

For charm Rochester was no Falkland. He has been described as of middle height, brown of feature and well-shaped. Whatever his attractions of person and character, or the lack of them, adherence to a principle is an attractive trait, especially if it be a religious principle. So great consistency is not always found in a courtier, and the hasty-tempered Rochester could, according to Burnet, on occasion prove himself "the smoothest man in the Court". Halifax called him "scarcely a gentleman"—certainly the Hydes were not an exalted family—and Sarah, Duchess of Marlborough described him as "consumed by petty vanity and love of trifling ceremonies". These were the comments of opponents. Rochester was always diligent in the public service. Always an active man, he died within an hour of feeling unwell. Swift tells us in the *Journal to Stella* that he had but a few hours before penned a letter to Lord Darmouth on cabinet business.

Rochester was far from being the *beau idéal* of Thomas Babington Macaulay, but the latter's judgment of him is not unjust:

> "He had excellent parts, which had been improved by diplomatic and parliamentary experience; but the infirmities of his temper detracted much from the effective strength of his abilities. Negotiator and courtier as he was, he never learned the art of governing or of concealing his emotions. When prosperous, he was insolent and boastful; when he sustained a check, his undisguised mortification doubled the triumph of his enemies: very slight provocation sufficed to kindle his anger; and when he was angry he said bitter things which he forgot as soon as he was pacified; but which others remembered many years. His quickness and penetration would have made him a consummate man of business, but for his self-sufficiency and impatience. His writings proved that he had many of the qualities of an orator."

Macaulay goes on to describe Rochester as "a Cavalier of the old school, a zealous champion of the Crown and of the Church, and a hater of Republicans and Nonconformists. He had consequently a great body of adherents. The clergy especially looked on him as their own man".

Rochester liked to appear as a patron of letters. He was a D.C.L. of Oxford University, and was elected High Steward in 1709. He contributed a preface to his father Clarendon's *History of the Rebellion*, which began to appear in 1702. In it Rochester presented much of current Tory opinion, such as a preference for the Navy over the Army, for standing armies had an evil name: to this day the Army Act must be passed afresh by Parliament every year. Rochester also gives his own view, akin to that of Bolingbroke at a later day, that neither Whig nor Tory had "the game in their hands" and that each must incline to the interest of the realm. This, said Rochester, "is the plainest thing in the world".

The dedication of the second volume, dated 1703, is to Queen Anne, and expressed a conviction held by Rochester and his Sovereign, and before them by King Charles the Martyr and his non-Catholic adherents, that the Church of England is the foundation of the English Throne.

CHAPTER THREE

Shippen

ANY MODERN "NABOB" who has witnessed the early stages of parliamentary government in the former Indian Empire is the better fitted to understand English politics in the eighteenth century. Parliamentary sovereignty is on the way, but has not yet been established. The Executive is more the agency of the Crown than the nominee of Parliament; the electorate is small in proportion to population and largely illiterate; the landed interest is influential; personal and territorial issues have great weight in the return of members to the Legislature; and every election is disgraced by misrepresentation, intimidation and the most shameless of corrupt practices. Other political issues tend to be obscured by the bigger question: for or against the dynasty in power, for or against the Government?

Just as many have thought of Indian politics as resembling those of modern Britain, so there are those who have regarded the constitutional and political strife of the seventeenth and eighteenth centuries as though it was the two-party battle of Gladstone and Lord Beaconsfield. Neither assumption was justified. In these centuries Whig and Tory are still inexact terms, more safely and more generally applicable to states of mind than to political bodies. They are rather opposing interests and philosophies than opposing political parties.

The Roundheads and the Whigs were men of greater or less substance—magnates and bishops, bankers and merchants. Their philosophy, whether Low Church or Dissenting, theist or humanist, was in keeping with themselves. The Tories were the smaller squires and the country parsons and those who served and followed them. Once, Macaulay admits, they enlisted the sympathies of the most intellectual, and Lecky records how under William the Third they kept "the sympathy of the country clergy, the country gentry and of the poor". As for Fielding's Squire Western, he hated all lords. "They are a parcel of Courtiers and Hanoverians—my daughter shall have an honest country gentleman." Other Tories were known because they kept the fasts of the Church, still prescribed in the Prayer Book but ignored by Low Churchmen then and by most Anglican Churchmen today.

The Restoration, it has been suggested, was a compromise between the organic society of old England and the commercial morality and increasingly secular individualism of the upstarts. The Revolution, precipitated by the narrow folly of James, hastened the destruction of the ancient and merrier ways. The Revolution owed everything to the Tories, but it was Whiggery which was its legatee. There is much truth in the profound if turgid pages of Karl Marx. "The 'Glorious Revolution'," he wrote, "brought into power, along with William of Orange, the capitalist and landlord appropriators of surplus value. They inaugurated the new era by practising on a colossal scale thefts of State lands, thefts that hitherto had been managed more modestly. These estates were given away, sold at a ridiculous figure or even annexed to private estates by direct seizure. All this happened without the slightest observance of legal etiquette. The Crown lands thus fraudulently appropriated together with the Church estates, so far as these had not been lost again during the republican revolution, form the basis of the today princely domains of the English oligarchy. The bourgeois capitalists favoured the operation with the view, among others, to promoting free trade in land, to extending the domain of modern agriculture on the large farm system, and to increasing their supply of agricultural proletarians ready to hand. Besides, the new landed aristocracy was the natural ally of the new bankocracy, of the new-hatched *haute finance* and of the large manufacturers, then depending on protective duties."

Whatever the administration of the day, the kingdom was substantially in Whiggish hands. The Tory influence and idea lived on in the magistracy and local government, in the parsonage and manor house. William the Third's interest in England was in her usefulness as an ally on the Continent; he believed in mixed Ministries and never formed one which was exclusively either Whig or Tory. But Dutch finance, Dutch favourites, Dutch gin and the land tax levied on the squires to pay for what only later became a national war, the Whig predominance in the House of Lords where most of the bishops were of that view, all portended the great Whig supremacy which was to endure until 1760. In this period England became more urbane, more secular, more polished and more wealthy. Aristocracy became more arrogant. Toleration increased, and from it sprang cynicism and indifference. Science began to gnaw, like philosophy before it, at the theological foundations of society. Prosperity and the fear of a default in the public funds formed a barrier against Jacobite adventure. The commerce and the wars of England expanded her Empire, and both Empire and homeland were soon to be transformed by the grimy power of a thrusting industrialism.

The philosophy of Shaftesbury's physician, John Locke, was characteristic of the age of the Revolution and after. Nothing could have been more destructive of the idea of a Christian order. For Locke, the object of civil government was the preservation of property, and property was no trust held for God and his people but "for the sole advantage of the proprietor, so that he may even destroy the thing he has property in".

England as a whole became Whiggish. The party distinction lost reality. The Revolution altered party theories. William was out of sympathy with the Whig politicians' attachment to parliamentary liberty; he had been up against that at home. As for the Tories, though they were a party with a high view of the Crown, they had little in common with the Protestantism to which the Prince of Orange was accustomed. William's Government would consist of moderate Whigs and Tories who recognized his monarchy *de facto*, and in opposition would be found extreme Whigs, non-juring Tories, Jacobites and "New Tories".

Anne, by sympathy a Tory, feared lest she be dominated by a faction and chose Ministries of a similar complexion. After 1710 the Whig predominance in Parliament was offset by the creation of Tory peers and the consecration of High Church bishops, but moderate Toryism was becoming akin to Whiggery, and it was in that year that Harley wanted to form a new party of "Neuters". Rochester at the close of his career drew attention to the paltriness of party allegiance placed beside the claims of the Nation, and Henry St. John, Viscount Bolingbroke, wrote in the *Dissertation upon Parties* of 1728 that " it is time to cast off the Delusion of Party and to be no longer satisfied with Names instead of Things".

From the death of Anne to the accession of George the Third the Whigs sucked the fruits of office. The wheel had turned right round since Shaftesbury's day; now the Court Party was Whig and the Country Party was Tory and dissident Whig. The Whigs were reliable supporters of William's war and they were the basis of the Elector of

Hanover's kingship in England. He continued them in their supremacy by means of the royal patronage. Bolingbroke thus rightly attributed the power of the Whig patricians to the power of corruption, but corruption was then necessary to a Crown which depended for supply upon a Parliament not yet sovereign. He desired that the King should be above party, although that meant that he must be either a constitutional monarch or else that sovereignty should reside in Parliament.

Bolingbroke harked back to 1688, but the Patriot King belongs really to the era before the Revolution, which he eulogized. The real Tory answer to Whig corruption and Crown patronage was the reform and extension of the franchise, which would have allowed a Tory party as well as Tory principles to become the possession of the common people. The man who saw this was William Shippen, a Jacobite without the advantage of exalted birth or even of a country place.

It is not over-fanciful to see in Shippen a forerunner of the Tory Democrat, typified by Benjamin Disraeli, or for that matter by Lord Randolph Churchill, and had he not entered politics in the era of Harley and St. John, had he been a conspirator rather than a constitutionalist, he might now be better known than Carteret or Chesterfield. Today, when the Tory party is freeing its system of Whiggish accretions, when its appeal is to all classes of the Queen's subjects against doctrines and policies as specious and disintegrating as those of the worst Whig Ministry, when the people should know more of the reforming and radical aspect of the true Conservative cause, it is right to remember William Shippen and what he stood for.

He was of the gentry of Cheshire, a Jacobite county, and his father was Rector of Stockport. An uncle became Mayor of Philadelphia. Save that he was born in 1673 and attended

Stockport Grammar School, there is little known of Shippen's youth. He went up to Trinity, Cambridge, studied law at the Middle Temple and was called to the Bar. In 1695 he married money, and the union did not prosper, for he was later separated from his wife, the daughter of Sir Richard Stote of Northumberland.

Nevertheless, the improvement of his fortunes enabled Shippen towards the middle of Queen Anne's reign to enter public life. In 1707 he was elected Member of Parliament for the Sussex constituency of Bramber in the interest of Lord Plymouth. Plymouth's son, Dixie Windsor, was brother-in-law to Shippen. Shippen was unlucky enough to be unseated on petition, but three years later was washed back again by the wave of feeling which sustained Dr. Sacheverell and brought the Whigs down and Rochester back to office. The cry was "Huzza for Queen and Church!" Everywhere "there was a violent torrent against everything that did smell of low Church".

Shippen became a prominent member of the October Club. Under William and Mary it had been a Jacobite coterie. Now it was the rendezvous of "high-flying" Tories of varied opinions. Shippen was less prominent so far in the House of Commons, though we hear of him soon after the Tory triumph as one of the commissioners appointed to look into the alleged peculations of John, Duke of Marlborough. He warmly supported two measures designed to preserve the Anglican character of the realm, the Occasional Conformity Bill and the Schism Bill, which Sir William Wyndham introduced into the Lower House.

It was not till the Queen died and the Tories were scattered in fear and confusion that Shippen became an opposition leader. In 1714 the Tories had power and the favour of the Queen. Power was lost through the incapacity of their leaders and the malignancy of circumstance.

Bolingbroke's *coup d'état* vanished into vapour with the death of the Queen. His comment was: "The Earl of Oxford was removed on Tuesday, the Queen died on Sunday! What a world is this, and how does fortune banter us!"

Not yet could a ministerial minority of the Privy Council decide the future of the nation. The Whig Lords like Shrewsbury were still very strong; as an organ of government the Privy Council was obsolescent but by no means impotent. "Fortune", wrote Swift, himself to be exiled for the rest of his life to a Deanery in Dublin, "turned rotten at the very moment it grew ripe." The Whigs imported the Elector of Hanover, and Bolingbroke, although he was to exert his influence, would never again hold office, if we except an unheroic term as Secretary of State to James the Third. So began a half-century of Whig hegemony and for Shippen twenty years of Jacobite leadership.

Not all his Tory predecessors' following adhered to Shippen. Some retired into foreign exile or to their estates; others were Tories with no stomach for a Catholic King, and it was not until after the Forty-five that Bonnie Prince Charlie had his flirtation with the Thirty-nine Articles. Shippen had perhaps fifty supporters and an ardent lieutenant in Hynde Cotton, the antiquarian Squire of Madingley. On occasions he had the backing of Sir William Wyndham's Tories and of disgruntled Whigs. The formation of a Jacobite party took time; the crushing of the Fifteen was a heavy blow. Shippen strongly denounced a Whig measure to grant a reward for the capture of King James.

In 1717 a General Election was due, and the Whigs introduced the Septennial Bill. It was therein provided that the existing Parliament should continue for seven years instead of the three years laid down in the Triennial Act of 1694. Thirty-one Peers protested at the disfranchisement of the constituencies, and Bishop Atterbury of Rochester, Protestant apologist and Jacobite, attacked the Bill with a fervour and violence more befitting a revolutionary agitator than a Spiritual Peer. He was both. When the Bill, which had its Second Reading in the House of Lords by a majority of thirty-four votes, was brought down to the Commons, it was Shippen's turn to attack it. Long parliaments, he cried, "would grow either formidable or contemptible". A hundred and sixty-two Members voted against, and the stock of Shippen rose.

The Septennial Bill became law in 1716. It was not long before Shippen was lodged in the Tower by the vote of his enemies. He had remarked of the King's Speech at the opening of the 1717 session "that it seemed rather to be calculated for the Meridian of Germany than Great Britain", and that " 'twas a great misfortune that the King was a stranger to our Language and Constitution". He moved an amendment, referring to the oligarchs' participation in the affairs of the South Sea Company, "to show the highest resentment against those who, abusing the trust reposed in them, had given so fatal a wound to public credit and enriched themselves by the plunder of the nation".

Shippen remained in the Tower until the end of the 1717 session. While he was incarcerated he received three separate offers of £1,000 in cash. One was from the Prince of Wales, the future George the Second, who, true to Hanoverian tradition, was in opposition to his father. All three offers were refused. William Shippen was no great orator—Horace Walpole said that he "spoke with his glove in his mouth"—and he did not become a statesman of the first rank, but his integrity was unshakeable and unquestioned. Pope writes:

> "I love to pour out all myself, as plain
> As honest Shippen, or downright Montaigne."

In a corrupt era Robert Walpole gave the verdict: "Whoever is corrupt, Shippen is not."

In 1720 Shippen returned to the attack upon the South Sea Company. He moved that their directors should be ordered to lay before the House the material upon which their dividends had been based, together with a list of their officials—"all of which boded not well to the Persons therein concerned". The debate went on, and Shippen gave his opinion that there were some men in great stations, whom in time he would not be afraid to name, who were no less guilty than the directors. Thereupon Secretary Craggs precipitated a general uproar by rising to the bait and to his feet and exclaiming that he would give satisfaction to any man that should question him either in that House or out of it.

It was Walpole, not the Jacobites, who profited by the bursting of the South Sea Bubble. Walpole had warned his countrymen of what would happen, and now they called him to their rescue. In those days friendship between political opponents was rare; Shippen and Walpole were friends. There was much in the latter which could attract the sympathy of a Tory. Walpole was no grandee or dissenting City parvenu but a Norfolk squire of old family and moderate means, who when the calls of State kept him in the metropolis hunted his beagles in Richmond Park. Like the Tories of the period, he wanted peace; it was war which led to his fall in 1742.

In 1720 Shippen had condemned as over-lenient Walpole's measure for the restoration of the public credit. Five years later he moved the reduction of the Civil List by £200,000, speaking of the King's "frequent journeys to Hanover" and of the "bottomless pit of secret service". Two years later, when the House of Commons voted a loyal address promising to enable George to "suppress all remaining spirit of rebellion", Shippen moved that the clause be added "with due regard to the Liberty of the subject, the constitution in Church and State, and the laws now in force". In 1726 he was attacking the Treaty of Vienna and that of Hanover as "for the defence of His Majesty's dominions in Germany" contrary to the Act of Succession. Shippen also opposed Walpole's Excise scheme of 1733 as "destructive to the liberties and the trade of the nation".

But by the seventeen-forties Shippen was less vehement to oppose. He was getting on in age; Shippen's friendship with Walpole continued. "Robin," he wrote of King George's First Minister, "Robin and I are two honest men; he is for King George and I for King James, but those men"—he meant Pulteney and his friends—"those men in long cravats only desire place under one or the other".

When, in 1741, the motion against Walpole was introduced, Wyndham was dead and Shippen and his followers walked out of the House, this in Lord Chesterfield's words, "broke the opposition to pieces". It was alleged that Shippen's action was the *quid pro quo* for the dropping by the Government of a charge against a Jacobite. It is more probable that the Jacobite leader did not want to vote against Walpole on a motion attacking him personally. To say the least, he preferred Walpole to Pulteney, and "would not pull down Robin upon republican principles".

Not much is known of Shippen's dealings with the King over the water. He steered clear of Atterbury's plots and took no part in the Fifteen or the Forty-five. Indeed, at the time of the earlier rising he found it necessary publicly to deny, by means of a declaration affixed to the pillars of the Royal Exchange, that he had played the informer. In 1740 Lord Barrymore was sent to Shippen by the Pretender and reported that as a plotter he would be too timid and ineffectual. Yet it was not timidity which brought Shippen to the Tower, and as a House of Commons man above all he was by no means ineffectual in his vindication of the Stuart claims in debate and by constitutional process.

To some contemporaries his position seemed anomalous. A Member wrote: "All your stuff about serving high church and monarchy is absurd, and your principle is self-contradictory and *felo-de-se.* For were it possible for your endeavour to succeed, and to bring about what your friends traitorously desire, your beloved church and monarchy would be destroyed. The event would unavoidably be popery and slavery." Tories themselves may regret the existence of a rival dynasty and that reproach of potential disloyalty which helped to keep them in the wilderness so long.

It is by no means certain, however, that a restored dynasty would have re-enacted the follies of James the Second, and Shippen neither intended nor would have abetted the imposition of the old faith or the enslavement of the people. He would have agreed with Disraeli in desiring "a free and independent people united with the Crown, buttressed by their institutions and able to resist a dominant clique who would enslave them". Shippen, like Disraeli, "never tires of protesting against control of the nation and its destiny by a single class".

He died, as he had lived his active years, a Member of the House of Commons. It was 1743. Had he been alive when Prince Charles Edward was arguing at Derby with Lord George Murray and the rest, would Shippen have acted to help alter the balance of British history? What influence might he not have used to work upon the wobbling New-castle? God knows. The Jacobite flame flickered out save in the hearts and memories of loyal men, simple perhaps more than gentle, and, though at the turn of the century Horatio Nelson was not alone in his affections, the general threat offered to legitimacy and monarchy by the ideas of 1789 and the bayonets of Bonaparte rallied Englishmen to the Hanoverian Sovereign who gloried in the name of Britain.

The Tory party was weakened politically, but was also enriched by the devotion of the Jacobite wing and their fortitude in great adversity. Their tradition can still inspire the willing subjects of Queen Elizabeth the Second. For this our thanks are due not to the intriguers and opportunists, not to the tipsy squires or White Rose sentimentalists with their ambiguous loyal toast, but to the men who were out in the Risings and to those who, like William Shippen, witnessed to their convictions more prosaically upon the floor of the Parliament chamber.

CHAPTER FOUR

Wyndham

JACOBITES LIKE SHIPPEN OR HYNDE COTTON who really meant what they said were exceptional men. Under the Stuarts Catholics had been Royalist, but few Royalists had been Catholic; yet their adversaries were capable of accusing them all of popery. The Bishop of Rome was anti-Christ, the Whore of Babylon, the Scarlet Woman and such like. The efficacy of No Popery as a slogan is not surprising when we consider the reigns of Mary and the second James, the wide currency of Foxe's *Book of Martyrs*, the Puritan dread of Irish armies, the Revocation of the Edict of Nantes and the flight of the Huguenots to England, the popular association of Christian and Catholic Majesties with foreign aggression and wooden shoes, when we reflect also that many Anglican observances, and observances shared by Anglicans and Roman Catholics, reeked to the Puritanical of the choking smoke of Smithfield. To call a Cavalier or a Tory a Papist was usually as untrue and as politically damning as is the modern trick of the Marxian Left of anathematizing their opponents as "fascist beasts".

After the Revolution high Tories could be condemned impartially as Jacobites giving allegiance to a Roman Catholic Pretender. To this day there are many who find a Protestant Jacobite an incongruity. Others associate the Jacobite movement almost exclusively with the Scottish Highlands. Yet men like Shippen were members of the

Church of England, and the English counties of Lancashire and Cheshire, with their feudal survivals and dim memories of the Pilgrimage of Grace, were Jacobite hotbeds. English and Welsh Jacobitism persisted not only among many of the smaller landowners but, as Sir Charles Petrie has pointed out, also among the lower orders, and King Charles the Third was shouted for by strikers at Newcastle-on-Tyne. This example of working-class reaction is paralleled in the Cromwellian period by the Diggers' proposition that William the Conqueror had "turned the English out of their birthrights, and compelled them for necessity to be servants to him and to his Norman soldiers".

Dr. Johnson, shocking Boswell not for the first time, told him that "if England were fairly polled, the present King would be sent away tonight and his adherents hanged tomorrow". But there was no chance of a poll of the people of England, and the law of High Treason was drastic enough to keep within bounds the dislike of very many Tories for a foreign dynasty and kings who knew not England or her language. Another strong deterrent was the increasing prosperity of the country and the efforts of Walpole, himself a country gentleman, to woo the squires by such measures as the reduction of the land tax.

Many in cottage, hall or rectory wanted to see the Stuart enjoy his own again. On the other hand, there was a natural feeling that there had been too much civil war already, that a restoration should be peaceful or not at all, and that a repetition of what had happened between 1685 and 1688 could not be tolerated. Therefore the claimant should either enter the Anglican fold or provide ample guarantees of its established rights and liberties.

Sir William Wyndham, the third baronet, is known as the leader of the Hanoverian Tories. Before that he had been a Jacobite. The traditions of his ancient and illustrious family were eminently monarchial. One Sir Thomas Wyndham (*obit.* 1636) gave the striking injunction: "I command you in all times adhere to the Crown, though the Crown hang on a bush, I charge you forsake it not."

William Wyndham (or Windham) was born in 1687 at the family seat of Orchard Wyndham, at Williton, near Minehead, the Somerset seaport. His father, Sir Edward, in 1689 expressed his opposition to the placing of William and Mary upon the throne. William's mother was Catherine, daughter of Sir William Leveson-Gower, Baronet.

One day, a story runs, the young William was returning home from a stag hunt. At the gate he found several of his father's servants clustered round a fortune-teller. He appeared to be deaf and dumb, for he was chalking the answers to the servants' questions on the bottom of a trencher. William would have ridden past, but the man signed to him that he would read his fortune. As often happens on such occasions, young William could not think of a suitable question, but the fortune-teller took the trencher and wrote clearly upon it these words: "Beware of a White Horse." William smiled and thought no more of it for a time.

In 1700 he was touring the Continent of Europe. At Venice in St. Mark's Place he fell in with a mountebank telling fortunes by means of a long, narrow tube of tin. Wyndham's curiosity was attracted by the fellow, and he held up a piece of money. The soothsayer at once directed his tube and said most distinctly: "*Signor inglese, cavate il Blanco Cavallo.*" ("English sir, beware of the White Horse.") Remembering what had happened before in Somerset, Wyndham thought that this must be the same fortune-teller. But the mountebank assured him that he had never left Italy and knew no language but his own.

William Wyndham was educated at Eton and Christ Church. In April, 1710, he was returned in a by-election as Knight of the Shire, and continued to sit for Somerset in every Parliament until his death. Dr. Sacheverell had recently been convicted on impeachment for his High Church, high Tory sermon on "The Perils of False Brethren both in Church and State". As we have seen, the mood of the people was in favour of such doctrines. The mob took out his horses and themselves carried Sacheverell to his trial at Westminster Hall. When a nominal sentence was imposed by Their Lordships, the bonfires blazed, the bells pealed, and not only Dissenters' tabernacles but Whig palaces were in danger of being sacked. The Ministry fell. Rochester came back, Shippen was returned for Bramber and Wyndham was re-elected.

Wyndham got the Queen's Buckhounds; his first wife, the Lady Katherine Seymour, daughter of the "Proud" Duke of Somerset, had influence at Court, which was later exploited in Bolingbroke's coup against Oxford. In 1712 her husband became Secretary at War.

Like Shippen, Wyndham was a leading light in the October Club, and he was among the founders of the Brothers' Club, of which Swift was a member. Wyndham spoke in the debate on the expulsion from the House on a charge of seditious libel of that other litterateur and satirist of the time, Steele of the *Tatler* and the *Spectator*. Steele described himself as Tory in Church matters and a Whig in matters of State. In matters of State he did not mince his language, but uttered "insolent, injurious reflections on the Queen herself", dictated, said her courtiers, "by the spirit of rebellion".

In 1713 Bolingbroke, the peace-maker of Utrecht, embarked upon his purge of moderates from the administration, the magistracy, and the Army and Navy, preparatory to seizing the throne when it should fall vacant. The *Examiner* began to prepare the public mind for a change of Tory leadership. Atterbury had been nominated to the See of Rochester; Bolingbroke's friend, Wyndham, was promoted to the Exchequer, and was picked for the headship of the Treasury which, Bolingbroke intended, should have the Earl of Mar, Atterbury, Ormonde and other Jacobites as Commissioners.

The favour shown to Atterbury was one of the means to the consolidation of the High Churchmen. Another was the Schism Bill, which Wyndham introduced in May. This measure, which also applied to Ireland, prohibited any man from acting as a public schoolmaster or tutor who did not receive the sacrament according to the Anglican rite. Repulsive to modern thought, it was in keeping with the Tory conception of Church and State originating before the Reformation. In the Commons the Bill had a majority of more than a hundred, but it only passed the Lords by seventy-seven votes to seventy-two; five Whig bishops opposed the measure. The Queen died before the Schism Act became law, and although it remained five years on the statute book not more than two or three Dissenting schools were closed. Two amendments were carried which are typical of the age. The first exempted tutors to noblemen's children, the second teachers of the three R's using the English tongue and instructors in mathematics "so far as such mathematical learning relates to navigation or any mechanical art only". Oxford denounced the measure and soon after was removed.

Bolingbroke's design of a *coup d'état* had the support of Jacobites and Tories. It had also been discussed with certain Whigs. They included Stanhope, Craggs, William Pulteney and Robert Walpole. The scheme died as quickly as Queen Anne. Wyndham's father-in-law and his Grace of Argyll were the Privy Councillors who induced the dying Monarch to appoint Charles Talbot, Duke of Shrewsbury, Lord High

Treasurer. Bolingbroke was forestalled; Wyndham was not present at the Council. The Whigs took vigorous steps to secure the Protestant succession in the awkward person of the Elector George of Hanover. Bolingbroke and Ormonde fled the country; Wyndham stayed in England. The subsequent General Election put in a Whig majority. Wyndham denounced the King's influencing of the electors by means of a royal exhortation "to have a particular regard to such as shewed a firmness to the Protestant succession, when it was in danger".

Wyndham was sailing close to the wind. In the summer of 1715 there were riots in London, at Birmingham, at Oxford and in the counties of Worcester and Stafford. Dissenters' meeting-houses were pulled down. The Tories spoke of *agents provocateurs* put on by the Whigs to complete their downfall. Ormonde and Oxford, who, like his opponent Bolingbroke, had been impeached, were universally toasted. In London persons pilloried for Jacobitism were protected by the mob from the usual horseplay and attentions.

From King James's Court in Lorraine came Allan Cameron, brother of the Highland chieftain, Lochiel, to spy out the land and to appraise the prospects of a rising. He met Wyndham, who saw to his return *via* Weymouth. Cameron reported that the English Jacobites recommended that King James should cross the water forthwith.

Unlike the Forty-five, the Fifteen was no less an English than a Scottish rising. The flight of Bolingbroke and also of Ormonde had left the leadership in the Southern Kingdom to Lansdowne and Wyndham. In Scotland were Arran and Mar. Lansdowne's place at Longleat was the centre of English conspiracy. Ordnance, small arms and swords were assembled at Bath. Further supplies were expected from France; there were always great expectations from France. Simultaneous risings were to take place in different parts of the West Country. Bristol and Plymouth were to be seized, and at Plymouth King James was to land.

When Wyndham appeared in Bath, which was to be the base of operations in the west, they rang the church bells and received him with every demonstration of Jacobite sympathy. Then news came from London that Lord Stanhope, the Secretary of State for the Southern department, had been given leave by the Commons to arrest six of their number, and that Sir William Wyndham was amongst them. Also marked down was Thomas Forster, junior, who led the rising in Northumberland until forced to surrender at Preston. Wyndham's nerve failed him.

His father-in-law also heard of the threatened arrests. He went to Court and offered himself as security for his son-in-law's appearance whenever he should be called. The Hanoverian, it is said, "in order to make the Duke easy", gave Somerset his royal word that Sir William should not be taken into custody. The Duke withdrew contented.

Sir William retired to Orchard Wyndham. But the Government was too uneasy and too well primed of Sir William's goings-on to allow themselves to be bound by the royal word. A day or so later a Guards officer, Colonel Husk, arrived to take him. It was about four or five in the morning. He succeeded in seizing some of Wyndham's papers, although the baronet tried to put him off the scent by offering the officer the keys of his escritoire. Wyndham was permitted to dress and to take leave of his wife, who was with child, and escaped through her bedroom window.

Next day he was recognized in an inn at Winton in clerical garb. The Government issued a proclamation placing a thousand pounds upon his head. Wyndham made for Surrey, where he wrote to a friend for shelter from the pursuit. The friend was from home, and his wife, terrified lest her husband become involved in treason and liable to its fearful penalties, lodged an information with Lord Aylsford. The servant who carried Wyndham's message was arrested, and on his person was found a cypher ring with a lock of Queen Anne's hair. The baronet went to Somerset at Syon House, Twickenham, and surrendered to his brother-in-law, Lord Hertford, who was a Captain in the Life Guards.

Somerset was enraged at the breaking of the King's word. He flew to Court and made resignation of all his places and emoluments. All the uniforms and badges belonging to himself and his servants in his office of Master of Horse he caused to be carried in a common dust-cart to St. James's, where he commanded his men to "shoot the rubbish" into one of the courtyards. "He could not refrain from making many virulent expressions against the King, and felt so great a disgust towards both the King and his ministers that he never appeared any more at Court until the next King's accession, when he was sworn of the Privy Council, and carried the orb at the Coronation."

Wyndham was conveyed to the Tower, after being produced before the Privy Council. As the chariot passed through the inner gates of the fortress, a painter was busy altering the Arms of Great Britain in accordance with the succession of the House of Brunswick. He was at that moment adding the arms of the Elector of Hanover—a White Horse.

Eight months Wyndham was held in the Tower. Then he was released on bail. He was never brought to trial. Somerset had the great influence of a great Whig, and before Wyndham's surrender to Lord Hertford his carriage had been seen at the door of the famous lawyer, Sir S. Northey.

Bolingbroke abandoned the Jacobite cause after the crushing of the Fifteen. "May my arms rot off if I ever use pen or sword in their service again!" He justified himself by the fear of tyranny, "for a change of religion would never be brought about by consent", and of the alternative, which, he declared, was anarchy. Stanhope had the Earl of Stair, King George's Ambassador in Paris, sound Bolingbroke with hints of possible Hanoverian favour. The exile undertook to detach his friends from the Stuarts, though, he added, he would betray no secrets.

One of the closest of those friends was "dear Willy", as he called Wyndham. He wrote to him in September, 1716, bidding him forswear the Stuarts. He arranged that the Government should see the letter first. Another letter to Wyndham, begun in April, 1717, and published after both he and the writer were dead, was an answer to the Jacobite *Letter from Avignon* accusing Bolingbroke of treachery as James's Secretary of State. In this manner did this stormy and profligate genius work his passage home to England and English politics. Wyndham, like Bolingbroke, came to accept the new dynasty. His conversion was doubtless assisted by his marriage into the family of a Whig magnifico; his second wife, Lady Blandford, was also a Whig.

In 1723 Bolingbroke's pardon passed the Great Seal, and when he reached London, King George sent him gracious messages, with the proviso that proper restitution would depend upon Parliament. Bolingbroke exerted himself to bring certain Tories over to Walpole. Nevertheless, the Minister was not surprisingly resolved that this formidable Alcibiades should not, if he could help it, return to his seat in the House of Lords. In time, however, Parliament accepted Bolingbroke's petition praying for the return of the family estates.

In 1726 the Whigs led by Pulteney broke with Walpole. Bolingbroke, who from the pages of the *Craftsman* castigated Walpole once a week, worked steadily for an agreement between them and the Tories headed by Sir William Wyndham. Shippen, for the Jacobites, although often in agreement with Wyndham, maintained his independence. Wyndham and Bolingbroke exchanged visits at Orchard Wyndham and in France. With Bolingbroke, Wyndham exhibited that humility which approaches greatness. He acknowledged his friend's superior talents and placed his own considerable gifts freely at the service of a chief, who, though he excelled Wyndham in brilliance, intellect and vision never equalled him in personal integrity or standards of behaviour.

This subordination of the leader to the genius must not allow us to undervalue Wyndham's place in English politics. Disraeli drew inspiration from them both. Wyndham's presence was superb, his hearing dignified. Like Demosthenes or like Winston Churchill, he had an impediment in his speech, but none the less became a distinguished orator. In *Sybil* there is mention of the "intrepid eloquence" of William Wyndham. With time his Toryism mellowed into liberality and showed itself, as it must in the true Tory, in an independence of narrow partisanship. His defence of the printing of parliamentary debates and his support in the national interest of Walpole's military establishment were attitudes which cut across those of the "high flyers". At heart Wyndham was less the politician and the party leader than the country squire; his heart was in Somerset.

When Bolingbroke had concluded the Treaty of Utrecht, Wyndham spoke in the House in its favour. In 1730 he moved a motion concerning the French failure to demolish the Dunkirk fortifications in accordance with the Treaty. Bolingbroke, whose agent Brinsden had been to Dunkirk to establish the case, was bitterly attacked by Walpole and Pelham in the course of the debate.

It was Walpole's policy not only to let sleeping dogs lie—his motto was *quieta non movere*—but by positive measures to seek the appeasement or the neutralization of opponents.

By permission of the Trustees of the National Portrait Gallery

Laurence Hyde, 1st Earl of Rochester

After W. Wissing

By permission of Lord Leconfield

Sir William Wyndham, Bart.

By Sir Godfrey Kneller and John Wootton

His refusal to repeal the Test was determined by his fear of a High Church revival, and the extent of his favour to the Nonconformists was the passing of Acts of Indemnity from the penalties accompanying those restrictions upon their freedom which he had no intention of removing. Even the great Excise scheme was to relieve the burden of taxation carried by the squires. The Tories, however, repaid him with no gratitude. It was dubbed "that monster the excise", and its withdrawal was greeted in Jacobite Oxford with the ringing of joy-bells and "King James and Ormonde!" Elsewhere the cry was "Liberty, Property, and no Excise!"

Walpole proffered his resignation to the King. Nevertheless, although two hundred and five Members of Parliament had voted against the measure, no compact was struck between Pulteney and Wyndham. The moneyed men could not agree to Tory demands for an increase in the landed qualification of Members; there were disagreements on foreign affairs; and the Whig opposition could not see its way to supporting Wyndham in his nominations for committees.

Walpole's system of government demanded a cohesive body of support in the House of Commons. The dismissal of certain placemen who were in opposition to the Court was therefore taken in hand. Among them was Lieutenant-General the Lord Cobham, who was Colonel of the King's Own regiment of horse, and one of his junior officers, Cornet William Pitt. In 1734 a vote of censure was moved on the score of these dismissals, but Shippen and the Jacobites would have none of it, declaring the motion to be a breach of the royal prerogative. It failed in the Lords by one hundred to sixty-two votes.

The opposition were not, however, to be halted in the harrying of Walpole, and they placed great hopes upon the bill to repeal the Septennial Act. Wyndham clashed resoundingly with Walpole in the debate. The Minister sneered at his arguments in favour of the three-year limit secured for a time by the Revolution Settlement, maintaining that in them he detected the master hand of Viscount Bolingbroke. Pulteney also complained to Wyndham of Bolingbroke's influence over him; his "very name and presence in England did hurt". In 1735 Bolingbroke again withdrew to France.

Next year Prince Frederick of Wales, to whom the King had long denied the rights and duties of matrimony, was married to the seventeen-year-old Princess Augusta, the Duke of Saxe-Gotha's daughter. The bride was chosen by George, who saw her at Herrenhausen. The Prince's allowance was enhanced, but no arrangement was made for his consort and, as the cost of his establishment was increased after the marriage, he complained not without justice of niggardly treatment. It is believed that Bolingbroke, then about to sail for France, urged that the situation be exploited. Lord Cobham's faction, known to Lord Hervey as the Patriots, to others as the Boys, agreed to take the question up. Amongst "The Cobham Cousinhood", based on the restored magnificence of Stowe, were William Pitt, George Lyttelton and the Grenvilles; Lord Chesterfield was their mentor, Bolingbroke their philosopher, and Wyndham and Pulteney were sometimes styled their two "Consuls".

Wyndham supported their motion moved in the Commons on behalf of the Prince by Pulteney and Sir John Barnard, but Walpole contrived to defeat the Bill by telling the House that His Majesty and His Royal Highness had come to a financial understanding. The result was a vote of two hundred and thirty-four against and two hundred and four in favour, Wyndham and forty-five other Members abstaining. As for the Royal Family, the unedifying incident ended in a compromise: the King unwillingly gave his assent to another Bill settling £50,000 a year on the Prince with a jointure for his Princess of the same amount, payable on Frederick's death, but the sum granted was less than the Prince and the opposition had demanded.

In the year 1739 the folly and incapacity of the Tories and other sections of the opposition were exhibited to the full. The fundamental difference between Shippen and Wyndham was a gift to the Court, and the Whigs were able to mark them both with the stigma of potential disloyalty to the Crown. Despite this, however, and despite the power of governmental corruption, there was now a possibility of turning the tables. Walpole was opposed to the approaching war with Spain and was inclined to retire, but the King refused to accept his resignation. His precarious position was improved by the decision of the opposition led by Pulteney and Wyndham to secede from Parliament. This solemn and futile farce was produced by Bolingbroke, who had recently reappeared in England; it failed to impress anyone, and was a most unparliamentary proceeding. Lord Cornbury, Sir John Barnard and other members of the opposition refused to participate. The field was left clear for Walpole.

Nevertheless his star was waning. The seceders returned to their seats, Pulteney claiming that their efforts had led to England's entry into the War of Jenkins' Ear. Detested by Walpole, the war was popular with the nation. Walpole was racked by gout and the stone and the clamour of his adversaries. "All agree", wrote Alexander Pope, "Sir Robert cannot live." The opposition centred upon Norfolk House, the residence of the Prince of Wales. George the Second was in uncertain health and the questions asked in 1714 were being asked again. It was at this time that Bolingbroke brought out *The Patriot King* for the private edification of the heir apparent and his party.

The title recalled the name given to the men of the

opposition. The book is a fervent protest against the prevailing system. "Good government", it declared, "depends on the unity of interest between the King and his subjects . . ." The King is "the most powerful of reformers, for he is himself a sort of standing miracle" and claims "admiration and love in every honest breast, confusion and terror to every guilty conscience, but submission and resignation in all".

Much of the book is more pamphleteering than serious politics. But it is important, not only for its effect on the future George the Third but for its rehabilitation of the monarchy in the Tory scheme at a time when the Court was the possession of their political opponents.

The *Patriot King* was one of the influences which swayed Young England and the young Disraeli. In the latter's *Vindication*, written in 1835, there is a striking criticism of the author and the book:

> ". . . in the present day, Whigs have become Reformers, and Tories Conservatives. In the early part of the last century, the Tory party required a similar reorganization to that which it has lately undergone." The man the age required was Bolingbroke, "the ablest writer and the most accomplished orator of his age. . . . Opposed to the Whigs from principle, for an oligarchy is hostile to genius, and recoiling from the Tory tenets, which his unprejudiced and vigorous mind taught him at the same time to dread and to contemn, Lord Bolingbroke, at the outset of his career, incurred the commonplace imputation of insincerity and inconsistency, because, in an age of unsettled parties with professions contradictory of their conduct, he maintained that vigilant and meditative independence which is the privilege of an original and determined spirit. It is probable that in the earlier years of his career he meditated over the formation of a new party, that dream of youthful ambition in a perplexed and discordant age. . . . More experienced in political life, he became aware that he had only to choose between the Whigs and the Tories . . . a choice between oligarchy and democracy.

From the moment that Lord Bolingbroke, in becoming a Tory, embraced the national cause, he devoted himself absolutely to his party; . . . and although the ignoble prudence of the Whig Minister restrained him from advocating the cause of the nation in the Senate, it was his inspiring pen that made Walpole tremble in the recesses of the Treasury . . . and eradicated from Toryism all those absurd and odious doctrines which Toryism had adventitiously adopted, clearly developed its essential and permanent character, discarded *jure divino*, demolished passive obedience, threw to the winds the doctrine of non-resistance, placed the abolition of James and the accession of George on their right basis, and laid the foundation for the future accession of the Tory party to power, and to that popular and triumphant career which must ever await the policy of an administration inspired by the spirit of our free and ancient institutions."

Disraeli found help both in Bolingbroke and in Wyndham. When, in 1832, he was advocating the restoration of triennial parliaments, Disraeli claimed to be upholding "the true principles, the just spirit of our admirable constitution, which had been asserted by the Tory Party in 'the most laudable period of its career—by Sir William Wyndham in a speech which for sound argument, close reasoning, and bitter invective, is, I think, unequalled', and by Lord Bolingbroke, 'one of the ablest men who ever lived'; and he was not ashamed to be as great and as destructive a Radical as Sir William Wyndham and my Lord Bolingbroke. . . . He was, in fact, 'a Conservative to preserve all that is good in our constitution, a Radical to remove all that is bad'."*

Wyndham spoke of the spell of the White Horse having been broken with his imprisonment in the Tower of London. It was not so. In 1740 he was out hunting and thrown when leaping a ditch. His neck was broken. Sir William was riding a white horse.

* Monypenny & Buckle, *Life of Disraeli*, vol. 1, c.xi.

There was buried with Wyndham in the Church of St. Decuman at Watchet the hope of a coalition based on Norfolk House—"the unholy alliance" of Walpole's fears. Walpole's Ministry was in collapse, but the scruples of Shippen gave the succession to Carteret. "What a star has our Minister! Wyndham dead!" Vainly and bitterly Bolingbroke fulminated against Tory disunity and folly. "If Wyndham", he cried, "had lived he would have hindered these strange creatures—I can hardly call them men—from doing all the mischief they have lately done."

His very death revealed Wyndham's value to the Tory cause. Von Ranke, describing Sir John Barnard, the Tory Alderman of London, writes that Walpole "ranked him one of his most dangerous opponents. Another was the Tory, Wyndham, a friend of Bolingbroke. Like the latter he had recovered from his predilection to the Pretender, and made it his object in life to give the spirit of the constitution room to develop above the ceaseless agitation of parties. With other Whigs he might perhaps have united, with Walpole never". With Shippen, it was the other way about. Such influence for ill and good did personal likes and dislikes then possess. "His well-grouped arguments," von Ranke goes on, "his clear expression, his personal dignity, won him always a favourable hearing in Parliament."

Speaker Onslow, a Whig, paid this tribute: "He was in my opinion the most made for a great man of any that I have known in this age, everything about him seemed great, there was no inconsistency in his composition, all the parts of his character suited. There was much force and dignity in his person and speaking and power that always animated himself and his hearers, and with the decoration of his manner, produced not only attentive and respectful, but even a reverend regard to whatever he spoke."

A true verdict is also given in Collins's Peerage:

"He was in person very amiable, and accomplished in all parts of fine breeding; well read in learning, and of a happy memory; of great honour and integrity, in every act of life; and strictly attached to the interest of his country. He was esteemed one of the best speakers of the House of Commons, where his eloquence was well heard. Mr. Pope has transmitted to posterity this character of him, among others:

> 'How can I Pulteney, Chesterfield forget,
> While Roman spirit charms, and Attic wit:
> Or Wyndham, just to freedom and the throne,
> The master of our passions, and his own?' "

CHAPTER FIVE

Burdett

THE WHIG SYSTEM OF GOVERNMENT was government through less than a hundred great families represented in both Houses of Parliament. The Whig power rested on royal patronage bestowed in the form not only of "places" for the landed but of contracts for the merchants. Votes in Parliament were a marketable commodity, and a gentleman could get his bread by his attendance in the division lobbies. The pocket borough was among the scandals of the system, but it did mitigate its exclusiveness by providing openings for a Burke or a Pitt whose promise was greater than his connections. The pervasiveness of the oligarchy was also limited by the Tory predominance in the countryside where squire and parson held the keys of heaven and the lock-up. There was also an urban Tory element, to some extent independent, composed of the parliamentary representatives of the City of London and certain other great towns.

Bolingbroke, the philosopher of post-Revolutionary Toryism, opposed the national ideal to the ideals of parties. The conquest of England and the soul of England by plutocracy had decreed the dominance of Whiggish views and blurred the distinctions of party doctrine. The dynastic question was settled by 1760. The spirit of the age was towards indifference and latitudinarianism in religion. The Establishment was largely Erastian, and, though fox-hunting and spirituality are not incompatible, the eighteenth-century squarson was of a different order from the Caroline divines.

As we have seen, the Walpole règime crashed with the peace to which it was so deeply attached. It lacked the popular and the moral support necessary for the conduct of the Continental, maritime and colonial wars which won England a new empire before she had thrown away her first one on the North American seaboard. The desire of many for national government was strengthened by the needs of war. Though a Patriot King were a dream, there was a demand for measures not men. Chatham thought of himself as above party. He was a national, not a party, personality. A Grenville Whig, he was also a disciple of Bolingbroke, and although it can be argued that he adhered to the traditional Tory "blue water policy" and worked for the acquisition not of vast colonial dominion but of forts and islands of strategic and commercial advantage, Chatham's achievements served to add Empire to the Tory pantheon. He was the solvent of what there were of genuine party distinctions; he resisted the policy, which had Tory and popular support, of denying to the King's subjects in the thirteen Colonies liberties which the King's subjects enjoyed at home. Chatham was a difficult person; he was often at loggerheads with the Sovereign he reverenced. The statesman who subsidized Frederick of Prussia was he who as an opposition member had denounced subsidies to Hanover. Perhaps Chatham was most Tory in his constant appeal to the judgment of the populace.

The victories of Dettingen and Minden, of Plassey and the Heights of Abraham were not the triumphs of Whigs or Tories but of the British arms and the British taxpayer. It had been possible for Tories to discountenance the wars of William of Orange and to remain a Little England party despite the general pride in Marlborough's victories; but by the time of the Seven Years' War the new ideas and the new economy of England had matured and become generally accepted. The first opposition to the wars of Chatham came not from Tory gentlemen fuming at the profiteers, but from Whigs fearing for the solvency of the National Debt.

The Tories had travelled a long road since the Restoration. With the succession of George the Third they were again King's men as well as Churchmen. Jacobitism was now either a great memory or a pleasing whimsy, and Farmer George was almost an Englishman. He turned their own borough-mongering system against the Whigs, and welcomed the support of bankers and contractors who had done well in the war. The old Tory gentry of the provinces were not always sufficiently responsive to the royal wishes. George turned therefore to the new rich, who were eager to climb into good society by way of Parliament. Among the most reliable of these King's friends were the East India Nabobs—men like Warren Hastings and many others less elevated and less undeserving of impeachment. To this alliance of Calcutta with the Crown may be attributed much of the undiscriminating attack which the Whigs made upon the rule of John Company in India. Later, the younger Pitt added to the Tories men of humble origin such as Addington, Huskisson and Canning.

The Tory Party is always right to seek new blood. It is wrong if it takes in with them men and ways of thought unequal to the government of a great country. Cobbett in 1802 protested against the invasion of the governing class by unworthy newcomers. "The ancient nobility and gentry of the kingdom have, with very few exceptions, been thrust out of all public employments. . . . A race of merchants and manufacturers and bankers and loan jobbers and contractors have usurped their place." The former party of the country gentry ranged against the great Whig families had been enlarged into an alliance of the gentry with the industrialists. In 1813 the Tory Lord Castlereagh, taking a rosier view of the change, was able to say that the House of Lords itself "was not of that aristocratic spirit that would deprive men of humble birth but of great talents of any participation in the administration of the State".

Toryism was now a broader force. That was to the good. It also became less Tory which was not. In the heyday of Whig domination the Tories would have done well to batter at the doors of oligarchy by pressing a demand for the reform of the franchise. As we have seen, that opportunity was lost, its advocacy confined to men like Shippen. The younger Pitt made the Tory Party a reforming party, while the Whigs stayed comfortably stuck in the mud. But his followers would have none of his measure for the reform of Parliament. The close of the century was a time of revolution abroad and defensive repression at home. The flame of Tory principle was damped down, to flare up again in the breasts of Radicals.

The times were not dissimilar to those remembered by people alive today. Both periods witnessed the consolidation of the governing classes against the insurgence of the lower orders and their allies from within the ruling classes. There was a general permeation of influences and ideas arising from foreign revolutions. In the first period it was those of the revolutionary Americans and French; in the second the Russian Revolution produced not only an aggressive revision of a subversive philosophy but counter-doctrines equally vile. By the time of the younger Pitt the Agricultural and Industrial Revolutions had loosened the fabric of Augustan society and caused cruelty which cried to heaven for reformation or revolt; in modern times that revolt which it should have been the Tory mission to guide in the ways of peaceful reform matured in extremes of redress which may prove to have weakened the whole body politic.

The most elevated Tory, or at least Conservative,

evangelist of the era of the American and French Revolutions was an "old Whig". In 1791, the year of the flight to Varennes and the triumph of the Gironde in revolutionary Paris, Edmund Burke, a Dublin Protestant with a Catholic mother, severed his connection with Charles James Fox and joined Pitt, as did other "old Whigs" such as Grenville, Spencer, Portland and Windham. Like Chatham, Burke stood for Libertas as well as Imperium. "The spirit which now resists your taxation in America is the same which calls all England on its legs, and by the Bill of Rights vindicated the English Constitution . . ."

But by 1791 French equality had become the headsman of liberty and a danger to the empire and constitution of England, and Burke appealed from the French to the English Revolution, and from licence to legality. He proclaimed the moral and spiritual foundations of society in memorable phrases which weather well:

> " . . . the State ought not to be considered nothing better than a partnership agreement in a trade of pepper and coffee, calico or tobacco, or some other such low concern; to be taken up for a little temporary interest and to be dissolved by the fancy of the parties. It is looked on with other reverence; because it is not a partnership in things subservient only to the gross animal existence of a temporary and perishable nature. It is a partnership in all science; a partnership in all art; a partnership in every virtue, and in all perfection. As the end of such a partnership cannot be obtained in many generations, it becomes a partnership not only between those who are living, but between those who are dead, and those who are to be born."

Burke and the Tories saw the war with the French Republic not only as a war to prevent the domination of the Low Countries by a single great Power but as the defence of English institutions against French anarchy. In 1807 the

Edinburgh Review divided "all civilized governments into free and arbitrary: . . . into the Government of England, and the other European Governments". The comparison was just.

The Whig rump were not alone in welcoming the Revolution of 1789 and the attempt to establish a constitutional monarchy in France. Fox found many to echo his approval of the taking of the Bastille: "How much is this the greatest event that has happened in the world, and how much the best!" But Fox and his following persisted in their sympathies despite the war and the Terror and the persecution of religion, despite the discipline of Bonaparte which made the "armed doctrine" of the French bourgeoisie the more dangerous to British safety and legitimate monarchy. The English war against Demos became a war against the Despot, but Fox ignored the change. Whereas Sheridan rallied to the Government at the time of the Mutiny at the Nore, Fox, speaking to Grey in 1802, rejoiced at the misfortunes of his country. "The triumph of the French government over the English does in fact afford me a degree of pleasure which it is difficult to disguise."

Against the slavery of revolutionary liberty Pitt stood forth as leader of the English "in defence of their laws, their religion, and of everything that was valuable to them as Englishmen". The repressiveness of his domestic administration is regrettable. It is also understandable. London, like Paris, had become a city of clubs, clubs with names such as "The Friend of the People", which associated them with the doctrine of the national foe. In the critical year of 1797, the Tory *Anti-Jacobin* appeared to counter the agitation of the pro-French; it was violent, but it was the voice of patriotism. It defended the interests and the traditional institutions of the nation, the product of long struggles and long experience, against the iconoclasm of ready-made alien philosophies. In its last number Canning describes a recurring type of English intellectual:

> "A steady patriot of the world alone,
> The friend of every country but his own."

Bolingbroke and Shippen and Sir William Wyndham would have been, and Sir Francis Burdett was, repelled by the severity of the Tory war government towards their opponents and towards unrest; but, where the eighteenth century had known the wars of kings, the Revolutionary War was a war of classes and peoples and philosophies. When the French threw down the head of an anointed Monarch as a bloody incitement to other nations they were answered by men who called themselves Whigs and Reformers. The sincere voice of Reform became indistinguishable from the ugly clamour of Treason. Patriotism became the gaoler of English liberty. "If any person", said Sir Samuel Romilly, "be desirous of having an adequate idea of the mischievous effects which have been produced in this country by the French Revolution and all its attendant horrors, he should attempt some reform on humane and liberal principles. He will then find not only what a stupid spirit of conservation, but what a savage spirit, it has inspired in the minds of his countrymen."

Thus the Tories resisted Reform and crassly resisted Catholic Emancipation, which was among the conditions of Irish fidelity. Tory cartoons depicted Magna Charta, the Bible and the Crown as the fountain of English liberties, menaced by the Foxite Whigs and their godless and popish confederates. Was not Catholicism the faith of the Irish rebels of '98 and own accomplice to "the infidel philosophy of Tom Paine"? It would be wrong to suppose that this Tory simplification was unpopular. In their prejudices the Tories were close to the common people, whereas English Jacobinism was less the evangel of the oppressed than the fashionable eccentricity of Whig aristocrats. The Lord George Gordon riots of 1780 had revealed the popular fear and misconceptions of popery, and it was a mob with the cry of "Church and King" which sacked the Birmingham house of the dissenting Dr. Priestley. Moreover, the Evangelical movement within and the Wesleyan movement outside the Established Church were both conservative and inimical to Roman Catholicism. If other Nonconformists incline in general to Liberalism, the Methodists have found nothing incompatible between Toryism and their religion. In 1804 Cobbett wrote in the *Political Register* that "there always was amongst the creature and close adherents of Mr. Pitt, a strange mixture of profligacy and cant: jobbers all the morning and Methodists all the afternoon". It is claimed for Methody that it saved England from revolution.

The Whig remnant were indulgent of Dissent, and the generality of Nonconformists leaned towards those who were most likely to win them civic rights and the reform of Parliament in their favour. In the Tory estimation therefore Dissent was subversive as well as heretical, and Loyalist Associations were formed by churchmen fearful of the threat of Disestablishment.

Behind the urban middle class demand for representation in the Legislature surged a ferment of economic upheaval to which Whig aristocrats and Tory landowners were in general blind or indifferent. The Glorious Revolution had brought in its baggage the modern banking system, and to the Bank of England set up in 1694 the Government of Dutch William had surrendered the sovereign power of issuing currency as a return for the financing of his wars. England conquered princes only to yield to merchant princes.

The claws of the capitalists reached out into the green fields. Three thousand Enclosure Acts received the Royal Assent in the course of the eighteenth century. The soil and the peasantry became the chattels of a few thousand landlords, who by means of improved and scientific methods of farming displaced for the new factories and the new slums the classes of yeomen and labourers who were to father the new proletariat of industrial England. Religion and politics now kept their station; they knew little of all this. They had not yet heard of the Condition of England Question. If liberty was the liberty of an *elite*, justice was for the protection of their property. Competition governed the workaday world; the right and duty to buy in the cheapest market applied also to the labour of human souls; and any idea of a just price and a just social order was blown to the sky by the economics of Ricardo and his like. The function of the law and the State and even the Church was not to see fair play but to check disturbance. Despite Edmund Burke, the English State became little better than "a partnership agreement in a trade of pepper and coffee". The enduring and organic nature of society was becoming submerged. It was a state of things of which Disraeli was to say: "The commercial principle now rules the country . . . if you convert the State into a counting house, it will not be long before the nation degenerates into a factory."

But the authentic Tory view of society was happily never quite extinguished, and in a period of Tory obscurantism and stagnation it was nobly and eloquently expressed in the life and speeches of Sir Francis Burdett. Disraeli tells us of "this very high-bred man, very tall and with a distinguished countenance. He was a complete Norman. . . . He was sprung from a Jacobite family, and entered life with the hereditary opinions of his class. He was against the Boromongers, that is to say, the new capitalist classes which William the Third and the House of Hanover had introduced; he was for annual Parliaments and universal suffrage,

By permission of the Trustees of the National Portrait Gallery

Sir Francis Burdett, Bart.

By Michael Archer Shee

By permission of the Trustees of the National Portrait Gallery

Benjamin Disraeli, 1st Earl of Beaconsfield

After Maclise

as Sir William Wyndham and John Hinde Cotton had been before him, in order to control and curb these classes. The latter (Sir J. Cotton) also was for the ballot. It so happened that the French Revolution was coincident with Burdett's appearance in public life, and so, in the confusion of circumstances, it turned out that he was looked upon as a Jacobin, when in reality he was a Jacobite." As Edward Coxe put it,

> "To make the wrong appear the right
> And keep our rulers in,
> In Walpole's time was Jacobite,
> In Pitt's, 'tis Jacobin."

Burdett's grandfather, Sir Robert, had sat in Parliament for Tamworth and been prominent in the Cocoa Tree Chocolate House, an assembly place of Jacobite politicians. The grandson was born in 1770 at the family house of Foremarke, Staffordshire. He was early a rebel. At Westminster he took part in a revolt against the Headmaster, Dr. Samuel Smith, who knocked him down with a thick stick. Francis Burdett was then expelled.

Oxford was followed by a tour of France and Switzerland. It was the ecstatic dawn of 1789, and young Francis Burdett was able to listen to the disorderly debating of the National Assembly in Paris. In 1791 he wrote some verses on the Revolution in laboured French. In 1793, the year of Terror and Pitt's First Coalition against those who practised it, Burdett, in the manner of an age accustomed to the alliance of land and money, married Sophia, daughter of Thomas Coutts, King George's Scottish banker. The wedding was celebrated at St. Martin's-in-the-Fields.

It was Coutts who thought of a political career as a cure for the moroseness which afflicted his son-in-law, and it was the Coutts money which enabled him to pursue it. The expenses of election were then ruinous. An election was not a serious revelation of the public will; it was a saturnalia and a sporting event. It was a circus for the plebs to be paid for by the aristocracy and the gentry, not only with money and largesse but by personal and violent contact with a rough and often angry populace. Elections were not democratic; but the liberties which the people could take with those who sought their suffrages—the freedom to sling mud or rotten eggs—were a sign of national strength sadly lacking in the *ancien régime* then in dissolution throughout Europe.

Three years after his marriage Burdett was returned for Boroughbridge in the Newcastle interest, and the Commons gained an exceptional orator. "It was all grace and music," Disraeli wrote. "Never was a more commanding manner or a finer voice. . . . His declamation was fiery and thrilling, and always natural. . . . He had considerable power of sarcasm, and his hits always told. His quotations were, I think, generally from Shakespeare."

Burdett joined the Constitutional Association for promoting a Reform in Parliament. This was a respectable, not a subversive, body. The Corresponding Society also stood for parliamentary reform, but it was a hotbed of republicans. Such Jacobin societies were put down as part of the general suspension of the Habeas Corpus Act. Burdett protested that it were better to repeal the Act altogether rather than reserve it for periods of tranquillity. Notice of any meeting of more than fifty persons had to be given to three Justices of the Peace. Were this notice not given, any magistrate could break up the meeting with the help of the military; he could, moreover, break up a meeting, even though the formalities had been satisfied, if in his opinion the speeches were seditious. The penalty for any breach of these provisions was death.

The unrest was economic as well as political. In 1795 wheat cost 75s. a quarter. The glories of the English Constitution were a mockery to the handloom weaver ruined by the mechanized factory and uncared-for by his betters. Bread rioting and the machine-breaking which appeared in 1812 as the Luddite agitation could not be prevented by legislation against public meetings and against Trades Unions. In the hungry countryside and in the kingdoms of the new industrialism reigned the police spy and the yeomanry. In 1797, the Navy mutinied at the Spithead and the Nore. That same year Burdett not only spoke in the House about Grey's motion upon the reform of Parliament, but assailed the inroads of the Executive upon the rights of the people.

Thirty-three of the Mutineers of the Nore were thrown into the Cold Bath Fields in Clerkenwell, a House of Correction built for the County of Middlesex by the Commission of the Peace. Some persons detained without benefit of habeas corpus were also among the guests. The best-known was Colonel Despard, an Irish adventurer who had seen service in the West Indies and was later executed for High Treason in conspiring to assassinate the King. The conditions of imprisonment, which included solitary confinement, were unspeakable. The prisoners could not be visited even by their wives. The cold could only be kept out by wooden shutters, which also excluded all fresh air. The plight of the prisoners was communicated to the outside world by messages written with skewers in tobacco juice or blood.

Burdett and two other gentlemen of his acquaintance determined to investigate, and the baronet, whose proud patrician visage and fearless unconventionality were a boon to the cartoonists, is portrayed by Gillray storming the Bastille of Cold Bath Fields. Burdett told the House of Commons that "when I took a coach in Oxford Road, I desired the coachman to drive me to the Bastille. 'Very well, sir,' was the answer . . . 'You know it then?' 'Oh, yes

I know it; everybody knows the Bastille in Cold Bath Fields'."

The Government ordered that a stop should be put to Sir Francis's inspection of prisons, but by 1800 he had succeeded in carrying a parliamentary motion for inquiry. The Commissioners' report, which mentioned disgraceful overcrowding and the bribery of jailers, led to a substantial improvement of conditions.

Burdett's hatred of tyranny caused him to collaborate with Fox and Sheridan. But he was never a Whig. "Both parties laugh at and despise the people." At Wimbledon, where he had taken a house, Burdett also became the friend of the bold Radical, Horne Tooke, and he resisted his exclusion from the House of Commons. Tooke had been an associate of John Wilkes in the pioneering days of the Reform Movement, but had quitted his Society of Supporters of the Bill of Rights when it appeared to have turned itself into a means of paying off Wilkes's debts. Burdett became Tooke's pupil in philosophy and philology. Both were Radical in allegiance. They were at the same time genuinely Tory in principle. Horne Tooke and Burdett subscribed to "the ancient principles of the Constitution", and Burdett had no use for Rousseau or Paine or any sort of *a priori* dogma.

In 1806 he met Cobbett and convinced him that "in the whole Kingdom there is not a man more attached to the Kingly Government and the whole of the Constitution of England". Indeed, one of Burdett's objections to the party system of his day was "that the prerogatives of the Crown are as much usurped on the one hand, as the Rights of the People on the other". Cobbett appealed to the age of monasteries and Merry England; Burdett went back to Runnymede and 1215.

Cobbett, Tooke and Burdett all attacked the savage

floggings inflicted upon the soldiery, Burdett unsuccessfully trying to obtain a parliamentary return of these punishments. In 1809 the militia at Ely became involved in mutiny on the score of their rations, that perennial and potent source of disaffection, and the culprits were lashed by the German Legion. Cobbett's burning denunciation landed him in Newgate on a charge of sedition. When he eventually emerged, Burdett presided at a dinner held in his honour at the Crown and Anchor Tavern and lasting upwards of six hours.

1802 saw the truce misnamed the Peace of Amiens and a motion moved by Sir Francis Burdett for an inquiry into Pitt's administration. In the General Election of that year he was put up for Middlesex to oppose Mr. Mainwaring, the Chairman of the Quarter Sessions who had most strenuously resisted Burdett's prison enquiry. The slogan of the baronet's supporters was appropriately "Burdett and No Bastille". When he was returned the *Ça Ira* was sung before Kew Palace. In 1804, however, Burdett was unseated for a time on petition, the proceedings dragging on for two years and costing him some £100,000 a year.

Cobbett on paper and Burdett in Parliament joined the attack on the Duke of York, whose mistress Mrs. Clarke was alleged to have done a roaring trade in commissions and promotions. The Government inquiry absolved the Duke, who abandoned Mrs. Clarke as a hostile witness, but his Royal Highness thought it proper to resign the Command-in-Chief.

In 1806 Fox died and Westminster became vacant. It was one of the few "open" seats, and, like Middlesex, had been a battleground for Wilkes. The Government candidate, Earl Percy, who according to Francis Place ran Burdett's campaign, proceeded to corrupt the electorate with bread and cheese and beer. Lord Percy's opponent, Paull, was supported by Cobbett and by Burdett, who subscribed a thousand pounds.

The Radical hope was defeated, but next year there was another election. Paull desired Burdett to stand with him and tried to influence his decision by means of a requisition from the electors. He wanted Burdett to contribute to the expenses and constantly badgered him for money. Sir Francis had declared his resolve not to fight any further contested elections, but went back on his resolve and offered himself as a candidate. He fell out with Paull and they fought a duel with pistols. Both were wounded and carried away in the same coach. Paull narrowly escaped an amputation. The committee threw him over and he received a mere two hundred and sixty-nine votes.

Burdett headed the poll, and the runner-up was Thomas Cochrane, a naval officer of chequered career and Radical sympathies, who fought not only in King George's service and in English politics but also in Chili, Brazil and Greece. The fight recaptured the fervour of Wilkes's day and was attended by the noise, violence, mirth, huzza-ing and rowdyism inseparable from elections at that time. When a dinner was held to celebrate the Radical triumph and to inaugurate an Anniversary Festival, troops were called out and ball cartridge was issued at Whitehall. Burdett was enthusiastically chaired by the constituents he was to represent for thirty years.

The Westminster Election was a victory for the cause of Parliamentary Reform which began to be asserted in the days of the Middlesex Election of 1768, was stimulated by the American stand for no taxation without representation, was approved both by Burke and by Pitt, but now had been relegated to Whigs and eccentrics like Sir Francis Burdett. The term Radical came to be given to him and others who believed that the House of Commons could never truly represent the will of the people until the suffrage was extended to all tax-payers or even to all grown-up men without exception. The notion that a woman should also have a vote was not yet canvassed.

Cobbett was the journalist of the Radicals. Sunday after Sunday in his *Political Register* he excoriated both the great parties in the State with impartial ferocity. Old Major Cartwright, mockingly named "the mother of parliamentary reform", and Henry Hunt, a Wiltshire farmer's son, founded propagandist societies and addressed public meetings in support of the movement. Hunt shared a room with Cobbett in jail in 1810.

Burdett's plan of reform resembles that of the Chartists, whom Disraeli was later to view with sympathy and introduce into one of his great novels. The baronet stood for the household franchise, more or less equal electorate districts, the holding of elections in a single day, and Parliaments of shorter duration. Cobbett in the *Register* denied that such a reform was the lever of revolution. "Pass a bill to this effect, and you need not fear Napoleon's gun-boats."

In 1809 Burdett brought forward a motion in the House in favour of the granting of the franchise to all tax-payers. That same year the Radical ranks were joined by Jeremy Bentham, a prison reformer on a greater scale than Burdett. His secretary, James Mill, attracted to the movement many of the younger intellectuals. They were a motley and talented party. Their political organizer was Francis Place, the London tailor who had managed the Westminster Committee.

Burdett had broken a Bastille in Middlesex. Now he himself was to be made a prisoner. An obscure City politician, who had been a Jacobin orator in 1792, and whose name was John Gale Jones, imprudently caused a small democratic club to adopt an order of the day protesting against the exclusion of strangers from the House of Commons. He was unceremoniously arrested for breach of privilege and haled before the Bar of the House. Burdett moved that Jones be discharged from custody. His motion failed, but his speech was revised and published in the *Register* and then repeated as a shilling pamphlet. In both forms its sales were immense.

Burdett in his turn was accused of breach of parliamentary privilege, and after much searching of precedents the Speaker issued a warrant for his arrest. The baronet refused to surrender save to superior force and from his Piccadilly residence wrote a letter dated 6th April, 1810, to the Right Honourable the Speaker. "Power and Privilege", he declared, "are not the same things, and ought not to be confounded together. Privilege is an exemption from Power, and was by law secured to the third branch of the Legislature in order to protect them, that they might safely protect the people; not to give them power to destroy the people."

Mr. Speaker Abbot was much exercised whether he could break open Burdett's doors and received small counsel from Lord Eldon and other luminaries of the law. Lord Redesdale suggested that resort be had to an Attainder, should Burdett persist in his refusal to yield himself. The Westminster mob began to gather and the Legislature received a garrison of volunteers. Lifeguards were posted in the streets. Francis Place and the Westminster Committee resolved that the military officers ought to be arrested by the civil power, should they refuse to withdraw their men. Four days after the issue of the warrant an entrance was forced into Burdett's house. He was found in the studied act of causing his son to construe Magna Charta. "I protest," he cried to the constables who arrested him. "I protest in the King's name against this violation of my person and of my house. It is superior force only that hurries me out of it, and you do it at your peril."

The route to the Tower was held by a thousand soldiers. The escort got off with a pelting, but on the way back after delivering their prisoner to the Constable of the Tower they were assailed with stones and mud. They rode into the crowd with carbine and sabre. Several died; many were wounded. A general massacre was averted by the acceptance by the troops of the City Marshal's suggestion that they should cross London Bridge and return to the Horse Guards by the Surrey bank.

Burdett was comfortably provided for, although a cartoon pictures him in the menagerie which was then a feature of the Tower of London waving Magna Charta through the bars of his cage. He remained in custody until Parliament was prorogued some weeks later. The hero's departure was less theatrical than his arrival. His constituents had planned a triumphal procession, but Burdett, who seems to have mistrusted Place, made a private exit and they had to make do with dragging an empty car to Piccadilly Place.

Burdett was re-elected for the City of Westminster in 1812. He and Cartwright concerted a programme of reform. Cartwright, whose Radicalism was of the most ardent, wanted equal constituencies and annual elections, to which Burdett agreed; but the Major also wanted manhood suffrage. This was too much for the baronet, and Cartwright dropped this demand in return for Burdett's assistance. Together they founded the Hampden Club, which was to be a proselytizing agency in the Evangelical or Methodist manner. The Club itself would provide a cadre of Radical leaders. Members were not only bound to pay the annual subscription of two pounds, but must also own land with a rental value of not less than three hundred. It was thus no Jacobin Club but a society of City politicians and aristocrats which included Lord Byron, Lord Cochrane and Charles Wolseley. Cartwright obtained thirty thousand signatures to a petition, and himself made a missionary tour of Scotland preaching the gospel of Radical Reform.

The General Election of 1818 again saw Burdett Member for Westminster. His two colleagues were Cochrane and Sir Samuel Romilly, later to be replaced by John Cam Hobhouse. In 1817 Burdett moved a motion for a committee on Parliamentary Reform; but progress was slow. In 1820 he again suffered imprisonment, together with a fine of £2,000 for his scathing animadversions on the Peterloo Massacre. Some eighty thousand people, largely of the working class, had marched to hear Orator Hunt speak on Reform. The magistrates used yeomanry and cavalry to arrest Hunt and break up the meeting. Eleven persons were killed and many injured. The Cabinet, Canning included, knew that the action was base and indefensible, but for the sake of order they defended the magistrates. Moreover, they brought in the repressive Six Acts.

The other great cause close to Burdett's generous heart was that of Catholic Emancipation. He was strongly against popery and as strongly in favour of justice. Pitt intended to combine relief with the Union with Ireland, but was compelled to resign in 1802. When Wellington won peace at Waterloo all sections of the opposition, including Canning and his supporters, were in favour of Emancipation. The Court and the country at large were resolute for No Popery. But the nation was no longer in peril, and the illiberal Tory administration could no longer invoke unity in the name of survival. In 1828 Burdett carried a resolution by a small majority asking for the Roman Catholic laws to be considered. As usual after a great victory the Army was weak; in Ireland, Daniel O'Connell's Catholic Association had attained formidable proportions. Peel and Wellington gave in, and the Roman Catholic Emancipation Act received the assent of King George the Fourth. With it came the break-up of the Tories and the emergence of a Whig Ministry pledged to the cause of Parliamentary Reform which Burdett had espoused when many Whigs were cold.

With the achievement of the reforms to which he had devoted himself Burdett became a Tory by party as well as by principle. That party now saw bad days. It had fallen to the Whigs to perform what to some eighteenth-century Tories had seemed essential to the overcoming of oligarchy; the war with Revolutionary and Imperial France had saddled the Tories with the defence of much that was indefensible. The Tory party gathered fresh strength when Peel and the Tamworth Manifesto opened Conservatism to the middle classes, but the old Tory philosophy was not to be renewed without Young England and another split in the ranks. It fell both to Burdett and to Disraeli to maintain the abiding principles of Toryism against the Tory Party of the day, to plead the cause of the people in the Parliament of the rich.

In 1835 Burdett's reconciliation with the Tory Party was resented by his Radical constituents. He resigned and was straightway re-elected, later sitting for North Wiltshire until his dying day. He was irregular in attendance at the House, but gave time to collaborating with Jeremy Bentham on law reform, thus earning the commendation of Hobhouse that he was the best constitutional lawyer in England. He was generous to good causes such as the Birkbeck Mechanics' Institute, and continued passionate in his devotion to fox-hunting, going out frequently with the Quorn and other packs. His attack on the Whig Poor Law of 1834 as being bad for the rich and bad for the poor was in keeping with the Tory tradition of a more Christian if less Liberal England.

When he ceased to trouble the established order the Radical Press denounced him as "a renegade", "in his second childhood", "a faded fox-hunter", "a poor worn-out old file bitten by the mad dog of aristocracy".*

Disraeli's judgment was otherwise. "The English public, which is particularly ignorant of history, joined in the taunts of his inconsistency when, late in life, the Boromongers having been got rid of, Burdett turned out to be what he started, a high aristocratic English politician.

"He was extremely vain, but not offensively so; his high breeding prevented that; and under all circumstances, he was distinguished by simplicity. I think he was the greatest gentleman I ever knew. For many years after he entered Parliament he rode up to Westminster from his seat in Wiltshire on horseback. The country, especially in that part of England, was then very open, and abounded in downs and commons. . . . He was very good-natured, especially to young members, but rather absent and thoughtless in domestic arrangements."

And again: "He was full of music, grace, and dignity, even amid all the vulgar tumult; and, unlike all mob orators, raised the taste of the populace to him, instead of lowering his own to theirs."

Burdett's integrity was complete. He was never diverted from his purpose by the lure of office. Three times he refused a peerage. He was consistent and unfailing in his reforming zeal. Grey was in the field before him in 1793, but he and his fellow-Whigs were but lukewarm Reformers when Burdett, Radical and Tory, was most active. The Whigs took over his programme; they never lifted a finger when Burdett was committed to the Tower. In the cause of Catholic Emancipation he was equally prominent. His work was an education for the people; in Sir Francis Burdett we find a lonely link between the old Toryism which had languished, and the Tory Democracy which was still to come.

* M. W. Patterson, *Sir Francis Burdett and his Times*, vol. 2, c.xxiv.

CHAPTER SIX

Disraeli—and after

"ENGLAND DOES NOT WANT to be turned into a spinning jenny, machine kind of nation." Thus Benjamin Disraeli, but this is what England largely became.

In the time of Sir Francis Burdett the Jacobin threat had been allowed to smother the groans of the poor and the cries of those who protested against their treatment. Instead of social responsibility, social repression; instead of freemen, proletarians; instead of *noblesse oblige*, the iron laws of supply and demand. An American cotton planter who neglected his slaves neglected his own interest; he was cutting off his nose to spite his face. But the Lancashire cotton manufacturer could treat Labour as expendable, for if he ran out of English workmen, there was always Ireland to draw upon. Craftsmanship yielded ground to blind toil. The tenure of property was often selfish and rapacious; the self-made master lacked as a rule the paternal instincts of the squire. Machinery grew always more complex, and with it wealth accumulated upon a small outlay of capital; but ruthlessness was essential. The manufacturer must be hard with himself, hard with his competitors, hard with his workpeople.

When the first reformed Parliament sat, children of six and seven were slaving under the lash. The efforts of the first factory reformers, like Sir Robert Peel, himself a mill-owner, were halting and timid in proportion to the problem, and their measures were readily evaded. Necessity drove parents to sell their children into the mills, and why not? Did not girls and boys work below ground in the coalmines, while their mothers were harnessed to carts and crawled beast-like on all-fours down passages a foot or two high? Well might Marx expose as cant the bourgeois eulogies of family life.

The industrial structure did not lack justification in the economic thought of the time. Economics has been well styled the dismal science. Malthus haunted the minds of men with a prospect even gloomier than the clouded skies of industrial England—the prospect of a land unable to maintain its rapidly rising population. The apostles of *laissez-faire* addressed themselves not to the humanity of men but to their self-interest. Suffering must not be relieved but by the slow working of economic laws, and if men died in the interval of starvation or typhus or cholera, it was because there were too many of them. Englishmen were not members one of another, and property and privilege had no duty save the pursuit of greater riches.

The year in which Queen Victoria ascended the throne was a year of bad harvests and bad trade. It was the year in which a group of Radical Members of Parliament and Celtic rhetoricians, following in the footsteps of Cartwright and Burdett, drew up the People's Charter, calling for the extension of the ballot from the victorious middle classes of 1832 to the labouring masses who had furthered their agitation. Annual parliaments, the abolition of the property qualification for Members and equal electoral districts were also demanded. This Chartist Movement was thus in descent from the Radicalism of Burdett's day; its members, however, were largely drawn from the working masses. The Whigs had carried the Reform, but it soon became as bitter a disillusionment as the Administration of Grey and Melbourne. The rotten boroughs had been done away with, but the borough franchise had been circumscribed, and it was owing to Tory efforts that there remained a popular electorate in the county constituencies.

The ameliorative legislation of the eighteen-thirties was the achievement of Tory statesmen such as Canning and Huskisson rather than of the Whigs, whose power, or much of it, now depended upon the manufacturers. The early factory reformers were Tories—Michael Sadler, Robert Peel, and Lord Ashley. The Whig reform of this part of the century was the Poor Law Amendment Act of 1834, which, in checking the extravagant compassion of rural justices who supplemented wages from the rates, made poverty a crime punishable with the workhouse. "That this Poor Law Amendment Act", Carlyle remarked, "should be, as we sometimes hear it named, the chief glory of a Reformed Cabinet, betokens, one would imagine, rather a scarcity of glory there." It is common fairness to add that the Whigs were supported in this measure by Peel, who, himself more bourgeois than the Whigs, was presently to sell the landed to the manufacturing interest and to destroy the ancient principle that the fiscal power of the State could be used for the protection of agriculture and the wider interests of the nation. The agitation against the New Poor Law was carried on by the philosophic Radicals and by a small group of Tories. Benjamin Disraeli was then a Radical and about to become a Tory.

Disraeli viewed the Chartists with understanding. In 1839 the National Convention, or People's Parliament, met in London. The People's Charter was transported in procession in a special vehicle to the Palace of Westminster. It carried a million-and-a-half signatures. Disraeli spoke in the Commons debate. He joined with the Whig Premier, Lord John Russell, in admitting the fallacy that political rights would cure social ills, but he denied that the Chartist

Movement could be dismissed as the work of professional agitators. The Reform Act had fathered the new Poor Law and the People's Charter, and the reformed constitution lacked the principle of the old, that "great duties could alone confer great station". Disraeli expressed sympathy if not with the Charter at least with the Chartists. They were his countrymen.

"I am not ashamed to say", he said in a later debate, "that I sympathize with millions of my fellow-subjects." Then, with a dig not only at Lord John Russell but at the historic Whig position, "The time will come when Chartists will discover that in a country so aristocratic as England, even treason, to be successful, must be patrician. They will discover that great truth, and when they find some desperate noble to lead them they may, perhaps, achieve greater results. Where Wat Tyler failed Henry Bolingbroke changed a dynasty, and although Jack Straw was hanged, a Lord John Straw may become a Secretary of State."

In 1838 Cobden and Bright formed the Anti-Corn Law League. The *venue* was, most appropriately, Manchester. Like the Parliamentary Reform Movement, this organization provided a diversion of that working-class discontent which the Chartists voiced. But its platform was as pernicious as the Reform of Parliament was necessary. The Cobdenite morality was perverse; the Cobdenite dogma was contrary to the national interest both in the long and the short term. To weaken agriculture is to weaken not only the prosperity but the defences of the realm, nor did the repeal of the Corn Laws cheapen the bread of the poor. The price of wheat continued to fluctuate. But the repeal was essential to the prevalent doctrines of Free Trade and the devil take the hindmost, and it symbolized the subordination of the country to the town and of British agriculture to British industry and commerce.

The *volte-face* of Sir Robert Peel meant that the leader who had rightly opened the Tory Party to the middle classes was willing to allow them to ride roughshod over that party's older supporters on the land. In opposing him, Disraeli was thinking not only of the squires but of "the population of our innumerable villages . . . the crowds in our rural towns". He meant also "that estate of the poor which, in my opinion, had already been dangerously tampered with". This great Tory, this great English, interest Sir Robert Peel wantonly threw away. He adopted a policy which was later not only to ruin our agriculture but to endanger the British industry and commerce whose interest it was designed to subserve.

As if prescient of our present difficulties Disraeli spoke of the American and the Prussian tariff. Were those countries who had profited by Protection to forego its benefits for the sake of Manchester? "They believe they can fight hostile tariffs with free imports." Such was the callous obtuseness of the Manchester School and of their imitators in successive generations. Such was the judgment of Sir Robert Peel, "faultless, provided he had not to deal with the future". What Peel wanted to "achieve is the cheapest. . . . But the wealth of England is not merely material wealth . . . we have a more precious treasure, and that is the character of the people. That is what you have injured". It cost the country the mass unemployment of the nineteen-thirties before any substantial measure of Protection was restored—in defiance of the Liberal Party and of the Labour Party which sprang out of it. One cannot but regret that Disraeli later decided that it would be imprudent and impracticable to reverse Peel's disastrous decision; at least by driving the Peelites into the arms of the Liberals he saved the Conservative Party from becoming another Liberal Party, and he saved it for the future.

The march of Chartism was halted by the Anti-Corn Law

League. 1848 was the year of its revival and the Year of Revolutions. In 1848 also Karl Marx and Friedrich Engels brought out their *Communist Manifesto* and warned the ruling classes of the day that "a spectre is haunting Europe—the spectre of Communism". This document was a specious, effective and not unjustly indignant indictment of the European capitalist order.

"The bourgeoisie, wherever it has got the upper hand, has put an end to all feudal, patriarchal, idyllic relations. It has pitilessly torn asunder the motley feudal ties . . . and has left no other nexus between man and man than naked self-interest, than 'callous cash-payment'. It has drowned the most heavenly ecstasies of religious fervour, of chivalrous enthusiasm, of Philistine sentimentalism, in the icy waters of egotistical calculation. It has resolved personal worth in exchange value and in place of the numberless indefeasible chartered freedoms has set up that single, unconscionable freedom—Free Trade. . . . It has converted the politician, the lawyer, the priest, the poet, the man of science, into its paid wage-labourers. . . . The bourgeoisie has disclosed how the brutal display of vigour in the Middle Ages, which reactionaries so much admire, found its fitting complement in the most slothful indolence. It has accomplished wonders far surpassing Egyptian pyramids, Roman aqueducts, and Gothic cathedrals. . . . The bourgeoisie has subjected the country to the rule of the towns . . . has agglomerated populations, centralized means of production and has concentrated property in a few hands. . . . The weapons with which the bourgeoisie felled feudalism to the ground are now turned against the bourgeoisie itself. . . . Let the ruling classes tremble at a Communist revolution. In it the proletarians have nothing to lose but their chains. They have a world to win. Working men of all countries, unite!"*

* Engels' translation.

The bourgeois Marx adored and loathed the triumphs of bourgeois expansion. Many from the Duke of Wellington down believed then in the imminence of social revolution; Marx believed in it all the time. But the wish was father to the thought, and Continental insurgence and English Chartism went into decline. The reason for this was not the redress of grievances by governments but the discovery of gold in California and Australia. This was indeed the greatest fillip to Western economic expansion since the Spanish exploitation of the treasures of the Indies. The effect upon English commerce was dramatic. English merchants controlled the trade of Australia and California, and gold poured into this country in return for the products of British factories. Trade everywhere looked up and abroad there grew a demand for the building of railways. The country which had invented railways and alone knew how to construct them grew richer yet. Thus was the swoop of the Free Trade nemesis diverted in mid-air; the hold of Liberalism was strengthened, the revolutionary march was halted, and Victorian England became prosperous, prim and imperial and increasingly humane.

But she remained Two Nations. The gulf remained fixed between them, bridged by philanthropy and not by a new ordering of their relations. Marx continued to believe that the gulf could never be removed except "by the forcible overthrow of all existing social conditions", by the violent victory of the wage-slaves over the bourgeois society which gave them origin. English Liberal optimism maintained that the salvation of society lay in the free operation of economic laws. For the mills of God they substituted the mills of industrialism, which worked considerably faster. But there was a third opinion as well. There were Tories who viewed the future of England in the mirror of the famous past and sought to reconcile the impressive advances of their time with the traditions and the harmony of older days. To the struggle of classes they opposed the unity of the Queen's subjects. They admired the diverse yet ordered comity of medieval and Tudor times, that happy marriage of rights and duties which was the ideal of days when the Throne had power to check the aristocracy and the aristocracy served to balance with their dignity of responsibility the pretensions of the third estate. Then the Church had the authority to enforce the law of love. Then the labourer and the craftsman could rejoice in pride of skill and lineage.

To that older society the young Disraeli and the Young England movement looked back, while their grasp of present needs and problems was more conspicuous than that of the prevailing Whiggery. Marx and Engels had to take notice of them, and the perverted Hebrew prophet could not restrain his dyspeptic resentment at seeing his half-true philosophy stood the right way up. The *Communist Manifesto* already quoted attached what it described as "feudal socialism; half lamentation, half lampoon; half echo of the past, half menace of the future. . . . The aristocracy, in order to rally the people to them, waved the proletarian alms-bag in front for a banner. But the people, so often as it joined them, saw on their hindquarters the old feudal coats of arms, and deserted with loud and irreverent laughter . . . As the parson has ever gone hand in hand with the landlord, so has Clerical Socialism with Feudal Socialism".

Marx's collaborator understood England more clearly. The range of his experience extended far beyond the Reading Room of the British Museum and the coteries of the Left. Like that other Jew, Disraeli, but more thoroughly than he, Engels studied the poor and their troubles at close quarters. The other nation of their betters he knew also; he did business with manufacturers and rode to hounds with the landed. In a footnote in that valuable work, *The Condition of the*

Working-class in 1844, Engels paid tribute to the "philosophic Tories, who have recently constituted themselves 'Young England', among whom are the Members of Parliament, D'Israeli, Borthwick, Ferrand, Lord John Manners, etc. Lord Ashley, too, is in sympathy with them. The hope of 'Young England' is a restoration of the old 'Merry England' with its brilliant features and its romantic feudalism. This object is, of course, unattainable and ridiculous, a satire upon all historical development, but the good intention, the courage to resist the existing state of things and prevalent prejudices, and to recognize the vileness of our present condition, is worth something anyhow".

Certainly maypoles and morris dancing were an inadequate answer to the challenge of the undocile poor, and the armour at the Eglinton tournament could not withstand a shower of rain but took cover beneath that most bourgeois of weapons, the umbrella. If Lord John Manners could perpetrate the couplet—

> "Let wealth and commerce, laws and learning die,
> But spare us still our old nobility,"

it was proper that the lines should be written:

> "Here comes riding my Lord John Manners
> With Roncesvalles upon his banners!"

But Young England was not an aristocratic clique with a mere rosy sentiment for the past. Though they wore white waistcoats, they were well received by the workers of Manchester, and in their desire for the union and balance of the estates of England, George Smythe and Manners himself conversed at length with manufacturers—a class which could have benefited by an injection of the feudal spirit.

Disraeli himself has left us a judgment of the movement in the preface to the collected edition of his novels: "They recognized imagination in the government of nations as a quality not less important than reason. They trusted much to a popular sentiment, which rested on an heroic tradition, and was supported by the high spirit of a free aristocracy. Their economic principles were not unsound, but they looked upon the health and knowledge of the multitude as not the least precious part of the wealth of nations. In asserting the doctrine of race, they were entirely opposed to the equality of man, and similar abstract dogmas, which have destroyed ancient society without creating a satisfactory substitute. Resting upon popular sympathies and popular privileges, they held that no society could be durable unless it was built upon the principles of loyalty and religious reverence."

Faith and nationality were the bases of the Young England philosophy. They were also the foundations of the Conservatism of Benjamin Disraeli, whose origins, and the complexion of his religious beliefs, were greatly different from his noble associates.

"I was born in the Adelphi, and I may say in a library." Benjamin's grandfather Isaac was naturalized in 1748 as "of Certo (Ferrara) in Italy" and D'Israeli is the Arab word for a Child of Israel. Benjamin claimed that his grandfather was "an Italian descended from one of those Hebrew families whom the Inquisition forced to emigrate from the Spanish Peninsula at the end of the fifteenth century, and who found a refuge in the more tolerant territories of the Venetian Republic". Of this there is no record in Venice, but the lineage of the D'Israelis may well be as princely as that of many an English noble. "We owe the English peerage to three sources: the spoliation of the Church; the open and flagrant sale of its honours by the early Stuarts; and the borough-mongering of our own times. When Henry the

Fourth called his first Parliament, there were only twenty-nine temporal peers to be found. Of those twenty-nine only five remain."

Nevertheless, the aristocracy of England was constantly, rapidly and rightly replenished, and to the aristocrats of his time Disraeli was an exotic adventurer, a member of a despised minority, in but not of the national community, a Jew of the first generation to be born out of bondage.

"Race is everything." It is as well that it is not quite everything. In England the race is mixed, the sense of nationality ancient and strong. Disraeli was a Jew and a great Englishman. His father, a litterateur of distinction, was concerned for books and not for ecclesiastical administration. When called on to serve his turn as Parnass of the congregation to which he belonged he declined to officiate and so broke with the synagogue. His son was baptized into the Anglican Church. This was fortunate and convenient. Disraeli remained a member of the Establishment throughout his life. At times the tradition and ceremonial of Rome attracted his ardent mind and spirit, but it was the vision of Jerusalem which gave him that universality of religious attitude which many Anglicans lacked, from the Supreme Governor down. It was Queen Victoria who vehemently declared that "it is natural that every one should have his own opinion especially on religion, but, when the policy of Great Britain comes into consideration *all* private feelings should be overruled".

Disraeli thought of the Christ as of a young Hebrew prince, come to fulfil the Law and the Prophets. Every Jew should be a Christian. Jerusalem came before Canterbury and before Rome. "The traditions of the Anglican Church were powerful. Resting on the Church of Jerusalem, modified by the divine school of Galilee, it would have found that rock of truth which Providence, by the instrumentality of the Hebrew race, had promised to St. Peter." So Disraeli wrote in 1870 in his General Preface to the novels. He went on to complain of the secession of Dr. Newman and others. That was going too far. The *Ecclesia Anglicana* was the nation in its spiritual garb, and for him the *Ecclesia Anglicana* was the Church by law established.

His association with Young England joined Disraeli, the Jew-Anglican, with Anglo-Catholics, who, without rejecting the Royal Supremacy, yet looked back to the pre-Reformation order. They wished not only "to change back the oligarchy into a generous aristocracy round a real throne", but "to infuse life and vigour into the Church, as the trainer of the nation". The Oxford Movement was the spiritual counterpart to the Radical Tory protest in the secular sphere against the inferior morals and the social enormities of the Liberal age. The men of Young England were Tories with a Jacobite slant. They rejected the Erastian tendencies of the eighteenth century in favour of the Stuart heyday of Anglican vitality.

Disraeli, however, did not go all the way with them. Smythe doubted his conversion to moderate Oxfordism which he compared with Bonaparte's conversion to moderate Mohammedanism. The truth was that Disraeli modified the Anglican tenets but in a different sense from that of the Puseyites. He could not fully share their medieval sympathies for "the Jews were looked upon in the Middle Ages as an accursed race". His emphasis on the Jewish origins of Christianity, which are undoubtedly most important, led him to blur the distinction between the morality of the Old Testament and of the New. His conviction, if mistaken, was genuine. The "superlative Hebrew juggler", as Carlyle styled Disraeli, spoke up in the House of Commons in defence of his race.

Despite his deviations Disraeli clearly saw that religion

without dogma degenerates into a mere system of ethics. So it has been since his day, with the result that the ethics also are in danger of death. "Remember, Mr. Dean," Disraeli said to the Broad Church Stanley, "no dogmas, no deans." Speaking at Manchester in 1872, he quoted the text, "in our Father's house there are many mansions; and I believe that this comprehensive spirit is perfectly consistent with the maintenance of formularies and the belief in dogmas".

This seems to be the meaning of the Anglican compromise. Ambiguous in its Articles, varied in its ritual, it gives much freedom of choice and judgment to the eclectic believer. The Establishment was not only "a guarantee of civilization", but "a barrier against history", essential to Disraeli as a national institution, sanctified by age as well as by its office. It was not to Bills of Rights that he attributed English liberty, but to the English character and English institutions. "Broadly and deeply planted in the land, mixed up with all our manners and customs, one of the main guarantors of our local government, and, therefore, one of the prime securities of our common liberties, the Church of England is part of our history, part of our life, part of England itself."

In the Anglican communion Disraeli died, attended by its minister. The latter paid tribute to Lord Beaconsfield's piety, describing how he "spoke twice on spiritual subjects, in a manner indicating his appreciation of the work of Christ and of the Redemption". But the death-beds of the great are the breeding grounds of legend. Mr. Christopher Hollis tells us in his book *The Two Nations* of two other stories of the statesman's end. The first was that "there came to his death-bed a priest of the Catholic Church, and he was there received a member of that enduring Body to which in his lifetime he had paid every tribute except that of submission. . . . According to the other—artistically perhaps the more probable—(for this Mr. Hollis is indebted to G. K. Chesterton) the watchers bent low over the dying man. They heard strange murmurings in an unknown tongue. It was the ancient Hebrew '*Shaman Israel Israel Adonai Ehod*'—'Hear, Israel, God, your God, is one God'—the oldest of all the professions of his race".

The East was the birthplace of Disraeli's ancestors and of the great religions. In his youth his Grand Tour took him to Constantinople and on to Cyprus and Syria, Jerusalem and Egypt—"the ancient land of Priestcraft and Pyramids"—and throughout his life his mind was constantly travelling through these golden realms. His great rival was altogether orthodox. Scepticism never tempted William Ewart Gladstone, the hero of Nonconformity and dis-establisher of the Irish Church, from the straight way of High Anglican faith. But what was Christian in Disraeli was clothed in different and more dazzling colours than was the religion of the majority of his countrymen. For him "the Church is a sacred corporation for the promulgation and maintenance in Europe of certain Asian principles".

Disraeli's social view is rooted in the Prophets and in Christianity. The presence of Two Nations was destructive of England because it was clean contrary to the Law and the Prophets and the Gospel, upon which the realm was intended to be established. God had become a stranger and a trespasser in the preserves of secular life. He subscribed to the Tory view that the Church is more to be trusted than the State with the education of children. He believed that State systems borrowed from China and Russia must alter the English character for the worse. He respected the Nonconformists—were they not Englishmen?—but regretted that because they disliked the Establishment they favoured the secular direction of education. Were Disraeli still alive he might well, in his conviction that dogma is essential—"no creed, no church"—comment cynically on the propriety and the logic of an agreed syllabus of religious instruction.

Born a stranger within the English gates, Benjamin Disraeli could scarcely suffer from insularity. He could address himself to English problems with that universal vision which has become rare since the sixteenth century schism but is yet present in the essential Tory tenets. Nor was Disraeli subjected to the somewhat narrow disciplines of a nineteenth-century public school. His mother felt most bitterly her Jewish race, and it was doubtless she who was most determined that her son should not run his head into public schoolboy persecution. He was sent to smaller establishments, but learnt as much at home. His father's literary knowledge and researches were immense, and his works were the admiration of Byron, Scott and Southey.

Isaac D'Israeli in his *Commentaries on the Life and Reign of Charles I*, and in another work on the first James, gave battle for the old monarchy against the Whig historians. His son did much to regain for the modern monarchy not its former active power within the constitution but its place within the hearts of the nation. In that sense the "real Throne" of the younger Disraeli's early desire was set firmly upright.

Isaac D'Israeli's son formed his first Ministry in 1874. The eighteen-seventies were a decade of anti-monarchial feeling. Why should the Queen cut herself off from her people and her duty, or have so much money to do it on? Radicals like Sir Charles Dilke and Auberon Herbert talked of a republic as less expensive than a constitutional monarchy, and in wider circles too it was thought that Victoria would be the last Sovereign to sit upon the throne. Progress must march onward. Like his father but in the field of action Disraeli set himself to turn back the republican tide and to save the Crown, "the only power that has no class sympathy". To do it he had to lay on flattery with a trowel. The Sovereign who had disapproved of this Jew-boy surrendered to his charms and gave him deep and affectionate approval. To her Disraeli presented the sceptre of the Moguls. The Throne became the token and the rallying-point of Empire, and in the age of confident Imperialism, spreading the bounds of England wider and wider yet, the republican spirit languished and died.

From the obscurity of the Adelphi to the Court of a Færy Queen is a transformation of the Arabian Nights. The trappings are more prosaic, the reality more splendid. The friend and servant of the Empress was a Semitic adventurer with oily ringlets. Lord Cromer called him an adventurer, adding that he was never a charlatan. Intensely sensitive, Disraeli was infinitely patient in pain and sickness, in adversity, in the long years of opposition and the wilderness. Ruthlessly penetrating in his appraisal of human beings and human performance, he could give all the appearance of heartless cynicism. He was neither cynical nor heartless because he dissented from the prevailing belief in man's increasing progress and perfection. Ambitious and satirical, Disraeli married for money—and loved his wife. He leaned heavily upon the society of women; he was passionate in his affections. "Never apologize," he would say, "never apologize for showing feeling. Remember that when you do so, you apologize for truth." No public school had taught him the virtue of a stiff upper lip and the unmanly vice of strong emotion. "I live for Power and the Affections; and one may enjoy both without being bored or wearied with all the dull demands of conventional intercourse."

The life of Benjamin Disraeli is a success story more brilliant, more romantic than any out of Hollywood. He told Melbourne that he wished to be Prime Minister, and after a very long climb he reached "the top of the greasy pole". The story is of inspiration to those who place the service of the realm before the amassing of money. Not the least thing about Disraeli was the extent of his debts. His career is a source of encouragement to all who embark upon the unplacid waters of politics, trusting perforce in their own navigation.

Disraeli by his life refuted the fallacy of determinism. He made the history of Victorian Toryism the story of himself. He changed the Party and preserved its principles. His personality, his courage and his abilities soared above the handicaps of class and period. The surrender of Peelite Conservatism was a surrender, to which Tories are often tempted, a surrender to the specious demands of the transient moment. Sidonia, the kingly Jew in *Coningsby* said this: "The spirit of the age is the very thing that a great man changes." Disraeli was a great man. He never dragged himself behind the conventions and the conventional nostrums of the age. "To govern men," was his conviction, "you must either excel them in their accomplishments or despise them." In this manner disadvantages were turned to advantage. Alien and exotic of blood and manner, foppish and eccentric in appearance all could be turned to charm and oriental glamour. He who lacked the sporting accomplishments of a gentleman could astonish the garrison of Malta by his declaration at the racket court that he had never thrown a ball in his life.

Not that Disraeli did not envy the cachet of those who were more systematically and conventionally educated. He did not tumble into the cheap error of decrying what was not his. Some work their way up by their merits and their efforts and add fresh vigour to the governing class. In England aristocracy has been strong, because it is an aristocracy open to the talents. Disraeli worked his way into their midst and subdued them. The novels reveal how the pomp and glitter of ceremonious society captured his hot imagination. Disraeli loved what was spacious and sumptuous. He did not reject those whose weaknesses and follies he saw so clearly and turned into literary fun. One of his ambitions was that of every middle-class parvenu—to become a landed gentleman and to own a seat in the country. It is an ambition as healthy as it is easy to deride.

The London-born Oriental became enrolled among those "magnificent asses", the landed gentry. As Squire of Hughenden he was regularly present in the family pew to read the lesson. He sat on the Bench at Quarter Sessions, interested himself in agriculture and the cross-breeding of cattle, and cared for the welfare of his tenants. He loved flowers. Gladstone liked to hack trees down: Disraeli preferred to plant them. All in all, the newcomer Lord of the Manor of Hughenden was no unworthy successor to Lord Chesterfield, Richard de Montfort and Bishop Odo of Bayeux who received it from the Conqueror. In 1880 he was writing to his intimate friend Lady Bradford like any gentleman farmer: ". . . Here we are absolutely ruined. The series of never-ending storms has destroyed all our hopes. A plentiful hay harvest drowned, and the finest crops we have had for ten years laid. It is a scene of ravage: of havock like a conquered country. No amount of caloric, of which there seems little prospect, could now rally things. It is quite heart-rending, and, coming from church today, my best tenants told me that they could struggle against it no longer. . . . This will be 'nuts' to Gladstone, who will never rest till he has destroyed the landed interest. If he were younger, the Crown would be in peril."

Disraeli believed in the institution of Property, but especially landed property. He knew that the loss of property is the death of liberty and that English history was too much the record of the progressive despoliation by the rich and powerful of the poor and the Church. That other Jew, Marx, saw all history as pre-history, because class had not yet been destroyed. Disraeli saw what Marx could not, that the enforcement of equality means the equal dependence of all upon an all-powerful government. The Marxian withering away of the State is nonsense, while men are sinful. Disraeli saw as clearly as Marx that institutions become misused and distorted. But he knew that to remove them would be to lose the precious experience of centuries of endeavour—to throw away the baby with the bath water. Power and privilege and wealth had become abused: they must again become a trust and the reward of duty.

Unlike the Tory philosophy of Disraeli, Marxism and Utilitarianism were both ephemeral doctrines stamped with the marks of class interest. What Disraeli said of Utilitarianism in 1833 is true of them both: "The Utilitarians in politics are like the Unitarians in religion: both omit imagination in their systems, and imagination governs mankind." Both systems claimed an absolute validity. Neither has withstood or will withstand the rush of circumstance. There must be a unity of classes and orders, a unity of Altar, Throne and Nation, a unity of the present with the future and the past. Tradition is diverse and it is folly to generalize about mankind. Disraeli's approach to human problems was therefore practical and empirical. His concern was not with the abstract Rights of Man nor with the rights of a class but with the actual rights of Englishmen, and with their duties in the world and to each other. Man is immortal, and Economic Man a travesty. Man must have bread, but does not live by bread alone.

By nature a Tory, Disraeli was not always of the Tory party. When he returned from his travels in 1831, England was rebellious and in distress. What party should he join?

The Tories were those who had resisted to the last the satisfaction of the Irish Catholics and their own middle classes, and they had been routed in a General Election and deserved to be. The Whigs were a Venetian oligarchy. Tories and Radicals should now drop their "nicknames" and join hands in a national party.

"My Lord, the Whigs appeal to the people, let us appeal to the nation." In 1832 Disraeli was a Radical and a Nationalist. "I care for no party. I plead the cause of the people." His mind was a revolutionary mind, his instincts and purposes were Conservative. A parliamentary politician needs the support of a party and in 1834 Disraeli joined the Tories, convinced that they must become the national party, a party of the people and of the monarchy which represents and protects the people. In the *Runnymede Letters*, which appeared in *The Times*, Disraeli showed that a revolutionary party was often illiberal, that the traditions and the institutions of a nation are the safeguards of its liberties and that as democracy increases so must aristocracy be maintained.

Disraeli was to revive against the tendency of a Liberal age the use of the State to redress injustice and to relieve distress. But he was not blind like a Socialist to the dangers of increased State activity and intervention. As he said in a speech in 1859, "if you establish a democracy, you must in due season reap the fruits of a democracy. You will in due season have great impatience of the public burdens combined in due season with great increase of the public expenditure. . . . You will in due season with a democracy find that your property is less valuable, and that your freedom is less complete".

"England", was Disraeli's belief, "should think more of the community, and less of the government." Her strength was in her parochial no less than in her national institutions.

"The local sentiment in man is the strongest passion in his nature. This local sentiment is the parent of most of our virtues." And again, "I have ever endeavoured to cherish our happy habit of self-government, as sustained by a prudent distribution of local authority."

"The Tory Party, unless it is a national party, is nothing." By the time of the Crystal Palace speech of 1872, the nationalist, not much interested in the colonies, had become the exponent of Empire. Under his leadership the Tory Party became an imperialist party. Its object must be to maintain our national institutions, to improve the condition of the people, and to preserve the empire. "The people of England, and especially the working classes of England, are proud of belonging to a great country, and wish to maintain its greatness. . . . They are proud of belonging to an imperial country, and are resolved to maintain, if they can, their empire. . . . They believe, on the whole, that the greatness and empire of England are to be attributed to the ancient institutions of the land."

There had, as Disraeli said earlier the same year at Manchester, been great changes since the age of Chatham in the position of England in the world. "The Queen of England has become the Sovereign of the most powerful of Oriental States. On the other side of the globe there are new establishments belonging to her which will, in due time, exercise their influence over the distribution of power. The old establishments of this country, now the United States of America, throw their lengthening shades over the Atlantic, which mix with European waters. These are vast and novel elements in the distribution of power." They were and they are. The great periods of Gladstone belong to the nineteenth century; the prophetic message of his adversary is apposite today.

Disraeli's imperial vision never descended into Jingoism.

In 1850 a Portuguese Jew, Dom Pacifico, who had been born in Malta but resided in Athens, had his house sacked by the local mob. Palmerston sent the Fleet to the Piræus; Disraeli was against such interference. Imperialists sometimes ignore logic and allow themselves to be zenophobes. Disraeli belonged to a cosmopolitan race which had suffered successive persecutions and survived. He was therefore sceptical of the efficacy of force as a means of controlling or influencing peoples and nations. "Ancient communities like the European must be governed either by traditionary influence or by military force." Disraeli favoured the former.

He joined with Cobden and Gladstone in defeating Palmerston on account of the bullying of China. To Disraeli an Indian was no inferior, but the heir of an ancient civilization. To Indian grievances he gave an attentive and a sympathetic ear. He preferred to think that we were in India by invitation, not by force of arms. "Our conquest of India in the main had been a conquest of India only in the same sense in which William of Orange conquered England. We have been called in—this happened very frequently in the earlier periods of our Indian history—by populations suffering under tyranny, and we have entered those kingdoms and principalities to protect their religion and their property." He might have added that the trade and property of the East India Company also required protection; nevertheless, there is substance in Disraeli's view of British expansion in India. When the Mutiny of 1857 was being suppressed with hysterical severity, he asked that justice should be tempered with mercy—"justice the most severe with mercy the most indulgent". Knowing as he did that "you can only act upon the opinions of Eastern nations through their imagination", Disraeli demanded the declaration of the Queen's sovereignty over India and the remedying of its peoples' grievances.

Earlier Disraeli had poeticized in favour of Federal Power as the spirit of the future. To Lord Derby he proposed the representation of the Colonies in a truly Imperial Parliament. He favoured Colonial autonomy, but there should be an Imperial Tariff, unoccupied lands should be secured to the Crown and arrangements made for joint defence.

The courageous and inspired decision to buy the Khedive's shares in the Suez Canal illustrated Disraeli's grasp of the imperial needs. "You have it, Madam." Always he looked eastward. What are now the white Dominions were then young, undeveloped, immature. England was an Asiatic Power; her leader an Asiatic. The Empire was an Indo-British Empire. London was the key to India, but the Empire's diplomacy and the Empire's expansion centred upon the Mogul capital of Delhi and the Government of the Imperial Viceroy. British influence was exerted from China to the Persian Gulf from Calcutta rather than Whitehall. In *Tancred*, written in 1847, Disraeli's character, the Emir Fakredeen, had prophesied how in India the Queen of the English would find "an enormous empire ready-made, a first-rate army, and a large revenue. . . . The only way to manage the Afghans is by Persia and the Arabs. . . . If she likes she shall have Alexandria as she now has Malta; it could be arranged". It was so arranged.

Not only the Suez Canal's purchase, but the handling of the Eastern Question, was largely determined by the needs of the Empire of the East. Always conscious of the influence of race, Disraeli dreaded "that Panslavist confederacy and conspiracy which has already proved so disadvantageous to the happiness of the world". Checked rather than stopped by defeat in the Crimea, the Bear ever groped towards the Straits and shuffled south-eastwards towards India. The Treaty of Paris ended the Crimean War but failed to obtain juster treatment for the Christian subjects of the Sultan of Turkey.

In 1875 there were revolts in the Balkans. In 1876 some twelve thousand Bulgars were slaughtered by Turkish irregulars—the *Bashi-Bazouks.* Russia and her partners of the *Dreikaiserbund*, Germany and Austria-Hungary, met in conference at Berlin. Great Britain was not invited. Russia and Austria discussed a partition of the Turkish provinces. For England and the Eastern Empire the integrity of Turkey was essential. The break-up of the Ottoman system could bring Russia to Constantinople.

Disraeli persuaded the Cabinet to agree to the rejection of the Berlin Memorandum which embodied the scheme of the Three Empires for a settlement. The British fleet sailed for Besika Bay on 24th May. On the 29th Disraeli wrote as follows to Lady Chesterfield: "Whatever happens, we shall certainly not drift into war, but go to war, if we do, because we intend it, and have a purpose which we mean to accomplish. I hope, however, Russia, at the bottom of the whole affair, will be sensible, and then we shall have peace."

Disraeli followed a clear course undistracted by the oratory of Gladstone, who had emerged from retirement to demand the expulsion of the Turks "bag and baggage" from the provinces they had desolated and profaned. In a speech at the Guildhall Disraeli, now Earl of Beaconsfield, gave Russia unmistakable warning. Great Britain demanded, as the best security for peace, the preservation of the territory and independence of the Sultan and the amelioration of the condition of his subjects:

"There is no country so interested in the maintenance of peace as England. Peace is especially an English policy. She is not an aggressive Power, for there is nothing which she desires. She covets no cities and no provinces. . . . But although the policy of England is peace, there is no country so well prepared for war as our own. If she enters into conflict in a righteous cause—and I will not believe that England will go to war except for a righteous cause—. . . she enters into a campaign which she will not terminate till right is done."

Such sentiments were not those of all Disraeli's colleagues. Lord Salisbury shared Gladstone's enthusiasm for the Turkish Christians and a sympathy for the victims of Turkish atrocities which Disraeli did wrong to belittle. But Salisbury did not share Gladstone's desire to help Russia against the Turks contrary to British interests and security. The Constantinople Conference of January, 1877, at which Salisbury was our representative, called upon Turkey to make concessions to the Christians. The Porte imprudently evaded compliance and Russia declared war. Great Britain remained neutral, but Beaconsfield issued a despatch which he afterwards described as "the charter of our policy" and "the diapason of our diplomacy". He warned Russia off Constantinople and the Straits, Egypt and the Canal.

The gallant Turkish defence of Plevna caught the sympathy of Britons who did not share the indignation of Gladstone and his supporters. The Queen and the "jingo" multitude were eager for war. Beaconsfield believed in peace through strength. In January, 1878, British men-of-war steamed up the Bosphorus and Beaconsfield determined to occupy Cyprus. Lord Derby, the former Prime Minister, now titular Foreign Secretary, a pacifist who was later to join Gladstone, resigned from office. Sir Stafford Northcote, the Chancellor of the Exchequer, noted in his diary: "We had some reason to apprehend a still more inconvenient advance to the coast of Asia Minor, where they might seize points which would threaten the Suez Canal and the Euphrates Valley and so intercept our communications." "In taking Cyprus," Beaconsfield commented, "the movement is not Mediterranean, it is Indian." This book is not the place to describe the Congress of Berlin whence Beaconsfield brought a peace for the Empire and for most of Europe, which was to endure for thirty-six years. The settlement which followed the Congress of Vienna lasted thirty-eight years, and "the difference," as R. C. K. Ensor says, "is not great enough to disentitle Beaconsfield and Bismarck to some, at least, of the credit which it has become fashionable to bestow on Castlereagh and Canning". Prince Bismarck said of Beaconsfield at Berlin: "*Des alte Jude, das ist der Mann.*"

The crisis from which Europe emerged at the Congress of Berlin brought Indian reinforcements to Malta. The Empire was a world force. The crisis had also shown that, England being the Empire's heart, the Empire must be defended in Europe and that any theory of Imperial isolation is the merest nonsense. Words which the Prime Minister uttered after the crisis have been resolved have a poignant significance for generations which have known 1914 and 1939. "One of the results of my attending the Congress of Berlin has been to prove, what I always suspected to be an absolute fact, that neither the Crimean War, not this horrible devastating war (between Russia and Turkey) which has just terminated would have taken place if England had spoken with the necessary firmness."

Vindicating his policy at the Guildhall in 1879, Lord Beaconsfield said :

"In assuming that peace will be maintained, I assume also that no Great Power would shrink from its responsibility. If there be a country, for example, one of the most extensive and wealthiest of empires in the world—if that country from a perverse interpretation of its insular geographical position, turns an indifferent ear to the feelings and the fortunes of Continental Europe, such a course would, I believe, only end in its becoming an object of general plunder. So long as the power and advice of England are felt in the Councils of Europe, peace, I believe, will be maintained, and maintained for a long period. Without their presence, war as has happened before, and too frequently of late, seems to me to be inevitable. I speak on this subject with confidence to the citizens of London, because I know that they are men who are not ashamed of the Empire which their ancestors created; because I know that they are not ashamed of the noblest of human sentiments—the sentiments of patriotism; because I know they will not be beguiled into believing that in maintaining their Empire they may forfeit their liberties. One of the greatest of Romans, when asked what were his politics, replied, *Imperium et Libertas.* That would not make a bad programme for a British Ministry. It is one from which Her Majesty's advisers do not shrink."

The dangers and preoccupations of the Eastern scene distracted Disraeli in some measure from the improvement of the condition of the people named as one of three main policies in the Crystal Palace speech. Even so much was accomplished. Moreover, just as "the greatness and empire of England are to be attributed to the ancient institutions of the land", institutions whose defence was another of those policies, so it was his third point, the preservation of the Empire, which was the object of Disraeli's foreign policy, and which, far more than remedial Acts of Parliament, secured the expanded livelihood of the people. The Empire is bread for British bellies. That is why Labour politicians cease to be anti-imperialist once they have taken office. In Disraeli's day, just as Liberalism denied that wealth and welfare march together, so it was the Liberal Party which resisted the policy of Empire upon which that welfare depends.

The indictment is framed by Disraeli himself:

"If you look to the history of the country since the advent of Liberalism . . . you will find that there has been no effort so continuous, so subtle, supported by so much energy, and carried on with so much ability and acumen, as the attempts of Liberalism to effect the disintegration of the Empire of England. . . . It has been proved to all of us that we have lost money by our colonies. It has been shewn with precise, with mathematical demonstration, that never was a jewel in the Crown of England so truly costly as the Empire of India. . . . What has been the result of this attempt during the reign of Liberalism for the disintegration of the Empire? It has entirely failed. But how has it failed? Through the sympathy of the Colonies with the Mother Country. They have decided that the Empire shall not be destroyed, and in my opinion no Minister in this country will do his duty who neglects any opportunity of reconstructing, as much as possible, our Colonial Empire, and of responding to those distant sympathies which may become the source of incalculable strength and happiness to this land."

It was the British Dominions which by their sympathy and initiative nursed the ailing cause of Imperial Preference. Its eventual adoption by the indifferent and tardy Motherland averted the economic collapse of the Commonwealth as a whole.

The defence of the Empire and of our institutions and the improvement of the condition of the people were one policy, not three policies. As for Disraeli's specifically social programme, it was commended by Alexander Macdonald to his constituents in 1879 in these words: "The Conservative party have done more for the working classes in five years than the Liberals have in fifty." Such was the case, although Disraeli presided over a Cabinet lukewarm in matters of social reform. It included Sir Stafford Northcote, a Conservative of the Peelite breed; Lord Caernarvon, who resigned in protest at Disraeli's policy; the "Little Englander" Derby, who called the Tory Reform Bill of 1867 which gave the artisans the vote "a leap in the dark"; and

Lord Cranborne (afterwards Marquess of Salisbury), who described it as "a political betrayal which has no parallel in our annals". Then, as in our own time, Whiggery was present in the inner councils of the Tory Party.

Disraeli himself believed that the health of the people must always be the first concern of a Minister. "*Sanitas sanitatum et omnia sanitas*" was his cry. A consolidating Public Health Act was passed and an Artisans Dwelling Act empowering the corporations of large towns to purchase land for housing. The Minister responsible was the Home Secretary, Richard Cross, a Lancashire businessman and lawyer. The inspiration was Disraeli. A Liberal Member scoffed at this policy of sewage. Disraeli replied that a workman, who had seen his children stricken down by fever, might see it differently. Other measures of social reform went through. The freedom of the Trade Union Movement was established in two Acts, the one making employers and workers equal before the law of contract, the other rescuing Trade Union activity in a dispute from the old law of "conspiracy". Legislation was also passed for the protection of agricultural tenants and merchant seamen.

The praise of the Labour leader, Alexander Macdonald, was well deserved. Another, Mr. Hyndman, of the Social Democratic Federation, decided to try and enlist the support of Beaconsfield for his own proposals for industrial betterment. He had read *Sybil.* Hyndman found the aged statesman tired and worn. For a while he sat silent. "Lord Beaconsfield," said the Socialist, "Peace with Honour was a dead formula. Peace with Comfort was what the people would have liked to hear."

"Peace with Comfort is not a bad phrase. . . . What do you mean by comfort, eh?"

"Plenty to eat, enough to drink, good clothes, pleasant homes, and sufficient leisure for all."

"Utopia to order? A fine dream, yes. . . . Not with the Conservative party, I assure you. The moment you wish to act, you will find yourself beset by a phalanx of great families, men and especially women, who will put you to rout every time. . . . This England, mark you, Mr. Hyndman, is a very difficult country to move . . ."

Tory Democracy was languishing. Its revival came from Birmingham. The torch of Young England and of Disraeli was taken up by Joseph Chamberlain. A Radical and a Unitarian, he was closer to Shaftesbury or Disraeli than to Cobden or Gladstone. As a Liberal Unionist ally of the Conservatives, he became the devoted advocate of the Empire and of Imperial Preference upon which depend today as never before the peace and comfort of the British people. "Joe" knew that Tariff Reform was the true means to Social Reform. The Conservative Party failed in both. The Liberal and Labour Radicals, imbued with Free Trade and Little England doctrines, found their answer to poverty and unemployment not in an expanding Imperial economy and the creation of new wealth, but in the transfer of existing wealth from the pockets of their opponents to the pockets of their electoral supporters. Lloyd George absorbed ideas of Henry George and declared war upon the landed aristocracy.

Already stagnant with Whiggery and a doomed Irish policy, the Conservative Party became increasingly diluted by frightened opportunists who perverted its principle to the preservation of their interests. In their hands policy became selfishness and folly. Only under the shock and stress of economic and financial collapse, of world war and of crushing electoral defeat did the Party turn back to a policy of Protection and Imperial preferential tariffs and revive the reforming spirit of Disraeli and of Tory Democracy.

If such terms have significance in our politics, true Toryism is less of the Right than the Centre. If Liberalism meant the subjection of man to money, Socialism results in his enslavement to the State. Toryism aims to check excess, to pursue the golden mean between tyranny and individualism. Both Tory Democracy and Social Democracy were opposed to the spirit, the operation and the effects of unfettered capitalism. In Tory Democracy was revived the paternal spirit of the Age of Faith; Socialism aims at a degree of State paternalism amounting in effect to an utter dependence of the citizenry upon their Government. Socialism, too, has something in it of the medieval; it is as rigid and as distrustful of invention and independence as was the society of the Middle Age. Socialism treats the man of enterprise as our forefathers treated a medieval Jew, that is as one who is only allowed to grow rich that periodically he may be plundered.

The Socialists aspired to replace the capitalist order by a classless society of equal producers. Their success has been limited to the conversion of capitalistic corporations into State monopolies beyond the control of Parliament and public. The workers in these nationalized monopolies remain mere wage-earners; but their employer is more powerful, more impersonal and more dangerous. British living standards are not the result of Socialism, but the fruit of enterprise and Empire upon which their survival depends. Socialism is an obsolete irrelevancy to the national problems. Socialism cannot increase the birth rate, people the Empire and refashion the defences of Christendom. Socialism cannot build a Grand Alliance of Commonwealth and Europe and the overseas territories dependent upon them. But only a political and economic combination of this scope and size, based upon national sovereignty and mutual arrangements of economic preference, can hold back the march of the Power to which Beaconsfield denied the Straits and free us from an ignoble subservience to transatlantic creditors. The old capitalism is dying, and with it will die the Socialism which rose up against it.

The concentration of economic power in the hands of managerial and bureaucratic groups is the result of the tendency to monopoly. This tendency Socialism professed to resist, but in practice has furthered and extended. The logical end is the totalitarian state. The alternative is not a return to *laissez-faire*, which is as impossible as the return to power of a Liberal Administration. The alternative is the distributist society, the democracy of property-owners. Power must be diffused before it devours us quite, that, well-spread, it may, like muck, do well. Workers must become partners and shareholders; industries must govern themselves. Local self-government and the autonomy of professional and religious bodies must be strengthened, not emasculated.

* * * * * *

The lives briefly studied in this book display the trend of Christian monarchy which runs through the pattern of conviction. In their expanding philosophy God takes precedence over Cæsar; the claims of religion overrule the contrary demands of the State and its functionaries; the "spiritual nature of man is stronger than codes or constitutions". Their Toryism is earthy of English earth, but its principles derive from universal wisdom.

The vistas of Disraeli and his successors are wider than those of Lord Falkland. The times are fraught with greater dangers. Man is suspended between the enrichment of his race and its destruction by starvation and scientific war. In the artificial and elaborate society of our industrial and Imperial nation, crammed in a congested and imperilled island, there is the hope and possibility of a general standard of welfare worthy of human dignity. But a balance must always be kept. The public provision of security and amenities must not degrade the family or the individual soul or impair the qualities of greatness without which England will go down in an Elizabethan travesty.

"It is certain", said Hilaire Belloc, "you must either restore the institution of property, or you must restore the institution of slavery. There is no third course."

FINIS

INDEX